OUT AT THE PLATE

The Dot Wilkinson Story

LYNN AMES

CHICAGO
REVIEW
PRESS

Published by Chicago Review Press Incorporated
814 North Franklin Street
Chicago, Illinois 60610
ISBN 978-1-64160-999-9

Library of Congress Control Number: 2023937994

Interior design: Preston Pisellini

Printed in the United States of America

5 4 3 2 1

To my dear friend Dot. With all my love.

Contents

Part Five: At the Top of Her Game

Part Six: Rounding Third

Part Seven: Heading for Home

Part Eight: Extra Innings

Author's Note

MY DEAR FRIEND DOT WILKINSON's life was incredible for so many reasons. It's not simply that she was one of the most decorated women's softball players, bowlers, and athletes of all time, nor was it the length of her time here on Earth—over a century—although any of these things by themselves would be impressive.

The magic of Dot's story is in the details. It's the tale of a childhood spent in poverty, an indomitable, unbreakable spirit, a determination to be the very best to play whatever sport she undertook, the independence to live her personal life on her own terms, and her extraordinary success at all of it.

Ours was a unique bond, forged out of loss and remembrance. Over more than a decade of countless lunches, visits, nightly phone conversations, research, extensive interviews, and discussions with her friends, Dot shared all of it with me. As she often told me, I know more about her than she knew about herself. She held nothing back, neither did she ask me to omit anything.

Now, at her request, I will share all of it with you.

Dot and Ricki, circa 2009. *Courtesy of the Dot Wilkinson Collection*

Part One

PREGAME WARM-UPS

1

Meeting Dot for the First Time

IT WAS A BRIGHT DAY in the summer of 2010 in Phoenix, Arizona. The air conditioning in my car rejected even the pretext of keeping up with the blistering heat. I parked on the street, turned off the ignition, and wiped my palms on my shorts. The television makeup already had melted to my face like a second skin.

"Here goes nothing."

I scrambled out of the driver's seat and strode up the driveway. The house was an unassuming, 1970s-era ranch at the end of a cul-de-sac. The desert landscaping featured several varieties of cacti. I noted a faded, hand-carved wooden sign next to the mailbox that read simply, WILKINSON & CAITO.

The Wilkinson in question was world-famous softball player Dot Wilkinson. In 1960, fifty years earlier, *Sports Illustrated* magazine had dubbed her "the female Yogi Berra." Her home state of Arizona named her the eighth-best athlete of all time, male or female. In her storied, thirty-two-year career with the PBSW Phoenix Ramblers, she'd achieved

All-American honors a record nineteen times, and her team had racked up three world championships. She was elected to the National Softball Hall of Fame on the first ballot in 1970. And that wasn't all: Dot was inducted into the National Bowling Hall of Fame, too, making her the first person of any gender to be elected to the national halls of fame in two different sports.

For weeks, I'd worked to secure a *Lynn Ames Show* exclusive, on-camera television interview with Dot and her great friend and teammate, pitcher Billie Harris. I'd met Billie, the first African American softball player of any gender to be elected to both the fast-pitch and slow-pitch categories in the National Softball Hall of Fame, a few years earlier. As my Internet-based television show highlighted women making a difference, I'd become determined to dedicate an episode of the combination talk/ talk-interview show to Dot and Billie and their remarkable legacy. There was only one problem: Dot wasn't interested.

After much cajoling by Billie and a personal phone call from me assuring Dot that I had no nefarious motives, Dot had finally agreed to sit for the taping, and we had arranged for me to pick up the two of them at Dot's house. The door swung open before I could ring the bell.

"I'm Lynn."

"I'm Dot. Come on in."

At five foot three, she was shorter than I expected, stocky and spry for a woman in her late eighties. Her gray hair, cut short and combed forward, had the purple tinge to it that sometimes happens to those in their twilight years. If she was aware of it, she didn't say. She sported a striped polo shirt, a pair of khaki shorts, ankle socks, and sneakers with Velcro clasps. Beyond a slash of lipstick, she wore no other makeup.

I said hello to Billie, who had arrived before me, as Dot led me down a short, tiled hallway. Every available inch of cinder-block wall space was papered with photographs she had somehow pinned to the concrete—Dot bowling, Dot playing softball, Dot and tennis great Billie Jean King at a Phoenix Women's Sports Foundation event, and Dot smiling and posing with her arm around various people I would come to learn were family members and friends.

I stopped before a wooden credenza cluttered with memorabilia.

"That's Ricki's glove," Dot said.

I turned to her. My eyes must've registered confusion, so she picked up the item I'd been staring at and elaborated. "They bronzed her second basemen's glove."

"I'm sorry to hear about her. How is she doing?" Billie had informed me that Dot's partner of forty-eight years, National Softball Hall of Famer Estelle "Ricki" Caito, had been hospitalized with severe complications from diabetes and congestive heart failure.

Dot's eyes clouded over. "Not good."

"I'm sorry," I said softly.

"Anyway," Dot said, changing the topic, "this is Ricki's Hall of Fame plaque and this one's mine . . ." She continued giving me a tour, pointing out the significant artifacts that occupied every surface. I recognized the evasion for what I assumed it was—discomfort showing emotions in front of a complete stranger—and focused on the series of plaques, trophies, and pictures. Her house was a virtual museum.

I checked my watch and regretted that I didn't have more time to explore the treasure trove. The camera crew and producer were waiting for us at the ball field I'd secured for the interview.

· · · · · · ·

Any reticence Dot might have felt before sitting down for our interview disappeared once the cameras were rolling. Prompted by my questions, she and Billie discussed challenging times caused by the racism Billie and the team encountered whenever they traveled, they laughed and reminisced about some of their zanier antics, and they shared the easy camaraderie of longtime teammates. Their personal connection, forged over the course of six decades of friendship, shone through.

In advance of the taping, the producer had suggested it would be a nice touch for me, Dot, and Billie to play a game of catch. I reminded the producer that Dot and Billie respectively were eighty-nine and seventy-seven years old. Still, once they'd agreed to do the episode, I'd asked both of them if they'd be amenable to tossing the ball around with me. I shouldn't have been surprised that they jumped at the opportunity.

As soon as we finished the formal part of the interview, we pulled out our gloves and moved from the shade of the bleachers to the steaming-hot all-dirt infield. I'd brought an old ball that had been languishing in my softball gear bag alongside the detritus of my own playing days. My battle-tested fielder's glove was an old friend. Remarkably, I was nervous. I worried about Dot's reflexes at her advanced age and that I could be responsible for whacking her in the face with the ball if she didn't get her glove up in time.

That concern was alleviated when Billie suggested that Dot and I stand at one end of the third baseline while she stood at the other. Dot would catch Billie's pitches, and I would throw back the ball so Dot didn't have to test her arm. The expressions of pure joy on their faces made it easy to forget that the cameras were rolling.

The rhythmic *thwap* of ball against leather, the scuffing sound of rubber-soled shoes scraping against the dirt, the resultant puffs of dust, the easy banter between old teammates and friends, Billie's spot-on delivery, and Dot's soft hands as she fielded those strikes: all these elements combined to make time stand still. So I was surprised when the director called, "Cut!"

"That was fun," Dot declared as we walked back to the car.

"I'm glad you enjoyed yourself. I brought you a little something as a thank-you for being a good sport." I reached into the glove compartment and pulled out a copy of my latest novel, a work of World War II–era historical fiction about the Women Airforce Service Pilots (WASPs). "I thought you might appreciate the story since it takes place around the same time you and the Ramblers were hitting your stride."

Dot read the back jacket copy. "Looks interesting. I can't wait to read it."

I tried to read her face and tone, but I couldn't tell whether she meant it or was simply being polite. I was just grateful to have gotten on tape what I knew would be a great piece of television. I dropped Dot and Billie off at Dot's house, thanked her again for the opportunity to sit down with her and Billie, and went on my way.

2

Dot and *Eyes on the Stars*

Two days after our interview on the ball field, my home telephone rang.

"Hello?"

"This is Dot." She enunciated the "t" with a firm, mid-range tone that belied her age.

Had I given her my phone number? I couldn't remember. And why would she be calling me? Was she having second thoughts about the show after the fact? Out loud, I stuck with the customary response. "How are you?"

"I finished your book."

I raised an eyebrow. "In two days?"

"Yeah."

I wasn't sure what to say. If she noticed the awkward silence on my end, she ignored it.

"I want to talk to you about it."

"OK." I drew out the "O."

"How did you know my friends?"

"What?"

"You wrote about my friends. I want to know how you knew them."

Briefly, I wondered if perhaps I'd misjudged how sharp Dot's mind was. "I don't understand."

"I had a friend who flew from Palm Springs. She flew those planes. How did you know to write her story?"

I furrowed my brow. "Dot, the book is fiction. I made up those characters."

"No, you didn't. I knew those gals. You just changed their names."

My cheeks flushed with indignation and anger. "I did no such thing. Those are not real people, Dot. It's fiction. I invented the characters and the plot, which is based on the real-life Women Airforce Service Pilots."

"Those were my friends."

"I assure you, while I did a lot of research, none of those main characters are real."

"Well, I knew them."

There was no sense in my arguing the point. "I don't know what else I can tell you."

"Have lunch with me and we'll talk about it some more. I want to show you some things."

Have lunch with her? Was this the same woman who had been so reluctant even to sit for an interview with me?

· · · · · · ·

By the time I arrived at Dot's house the next day, I'd set aside my indignation about her reaction to *Eyes on the Stars*. After all, the fact that Dot, who had lived through World War II, connected strongly enough with my characters to believe they were real was the highest form of flattery, wasn't it?

"I want to show you something," Dot said, without preamble. That was her style, I was learning: direct, economical, no frills or polish.

She led me a short distance down the hall. She stopped in front of a large framed, colorized, and posed photo of a very attractive ballplayer.

"That's Kay Rohrer. Heck of a ballplayer. She died young—thirty-nine. Breast cancer. She was a Hollywood movie star. She's the one who told me she flew those planes out of Palm Springs during the war, just like you wrote about in your book. You made me cry, by the way."

"I did?"

"Those women in your book were my friends; it took me back to those days. So many of my friends are gone now. I miss them."

"You understand that I made up Jessie and Claudia, right?"

Dot chuckled. "I understand that *you* believe that." Her blue eyes twinkled mischievously. "But to me, they were real."

Next, we went into a sunroom just off the hallway. Sliding glass doors led to a backyard pool. An organ sat silent against one wall, a couch took up space on the adjacent wall, and a large dining room table crowded the middle of the room. We sat at the table, and Dot slid a large scrapbook in front of me. "I think you might want to see this."

The book was well-worn, tattered, and stuffed to bursting with newspaper articles yellowed with age. For a history geek and journalist like me, an artifact like this was priceless. I touched it reverently and gazed up at Dot. Something in her expression told me that I'd passed an invisible test I hadn't known I was taking.

I opened to a random page. The headline atop the aged newspaper photo read, RAMBLERS RETURN FROM METROPOLITAN SOFTBALL FORAY.

There was Dot, second from the left, squatting with four other teammates, all dressed in cowboy outfits, replete with boots and hats. Dot's attention rested squarely on a woman pretending to pitch a softball. Another row of young women sat on a ledge above the Ramblers. Some of them stared at the camera, others at the pitcher. Intrigued, I read the photo caption:

> *The PBSW Ramblers, Arizona girls softball champions, were expected to return home early today after competing in the national tourney in Chicago and appearing in two games in New York's famous Madison Square Garden before record-breaking crowds. The Ramblers were*

semifinalists in the Chicago tourney and registered two victories over the Roverettes, one of Gotham's outstanding girls teams. Members of the Phoenix squad are pictured on the roof of the Radio City Music Hall in Rockefeller Center, New York, where they were shown dance steps by the Rockettes, world-famous precision dancers. The Ramblers reciprocated by showing Emilia Sherman, captain of the Rockettes, a few softball tricks. Louise Miller, cocaptain of the local squad and one of the West's leading hurlers, is doing the demonstrating.

I tore my eyes away from the photo. "You played softball in Madison Square Garden? And met the Rockettes?"

"Yeah. They were a fun bunch. Legs for days."

"You posed with the Rockettes on the roof of Radio City Music Hall?" I knew I sounded dumb, repeating myself, but . . ."What year was this?"

"1938."

I blinked and again took in the details of the photo. "How old were you?"

"Sixteen."

"Six . . ." My voice trailed off.

"That was an interesting trip. Ford Hoffman, our manager, had to buy us all sneakers because we couldn't wear our metal cleats on the terrazzo floor. Those Yankees had never seen anything like us. We paraded out onto the field in our cowboy outfits and the crowd went wild—12,500 fans, the largest crowd ever to see a softball game indoors."

"You played in front of 12,500 people in Madison Square Garden?"

"We stripped off the cowboy outfits and had our usual satin uniform shorts and tops underneath."

"It didn't bother you to wear those short shorts to play?"

"Nah. We loved those outfits; we had new ones custom-made for us every season."

"Your legs must've been a mess from sliding with no protection."

"We didn't care about that." Dot waved me off. "Anyway, we won that game. I think it was in extra innings. I know the game the next night went

Ramblers Return From Metropolitan Softball Foray

The PBSW Ramblers, Arizona girls softball champions, were expected to return home early today after competing in the national | ing girls teams. Members of the Phoenix squad are pictured on the roof of the Radio City Music Hall in Rockefeller Center, New York where they were shown dance steps by the Rockettes world

Publicity photo printed in the September 20, 1938, edition of the *Arizona Republic*. This yellowed newspaper clipping from Dot's aging scrapbook provided the spark and impetus for this biography.

Courtesy of the Dot Wilkinson Collection

eighteen innings. We won that one too, and the crowd was even bigger than the night before—13,500."

The idea of a women's softball game attracting that many fans boggled my mind. That it happened twice in a row, in one of the most storied athletic facilities in the world, and in 1938, was more than I could process.

"So where do the Rockettes figure into all this?"

"We were in New York for two games on consecutive nights, so Ford arranged some entertainment for us during the day in between the games. I remember that we went to city hall, where we met Mayor Fiorello

LaGuardia's secretary. She took us on a tour of the World's Fair grounds. Then we had lunch at Jack Dempsey's restaurant, across the street from the Garden. The burger was really good."

"World Heavyweight Champion Jack Dempsey? That Jack Dempsey?"

"Yeah. He ate with us and took a picture with me."

I shook my head in disbelief. Dot relayed the story as if everyone in the world had such experiences every day.

"After lunch, we went over to Radio City Music Hall to do the thing with the Rockettes. Then we went to the Polo Grounds for the Pirates–New York Giants game."

"Wow."

"I wasn't that impressed. I just wanted to play ball," Dot said, laughing. "One good thing that happened that night—I had an uncle who played the organ at a church. He was my mother's brother. I guess my mother wrote to him and told him I was going to be there. He came to the game, and I got to see him. That was really a great thing for me. That was the first time I ever met him. It was quite a thrill."

Dot got up from her chair. "I'm hungry. Are you ready to go get some lunch?"

"Sure." I glanced back over my shoulder at the scrapbook and imagined how many more treasures might lie within.

As if reading my mind, Dot said, "Don't worry. You can look at it again when we get back. In the meantime, I want to talk more about my new friends, Jessie and Claudia."

I suppose that was the moment. Dot was hooked on my fiction, and I was riveted by her life story—a match made in heaven.

3

Dot & Ricki

I PICKED UP DOT AT 11:30 AM. This was our second lunch date in as many weeks, again initiated by a phone call from her. She'd reread *Eyes on the Stars* twice more. I felt compelled to tell her that I *did* have other published novels she could read. Surely she must have memorized everything about Jessie and Claudia by now. She laughed and challenged me to bring her anything she could love as much as that book.

Dot greeted me at the door with a kiss, which caught me off guard. Apparently, we were now *those* kinds of friends. "Well, what have you got?"

I recovered my composure. "I figured you should start at the beginning, so this is *The Price of Fame*, the first book I wrote. I hope you like it." I handed her the book.

"I'll let you know."

I laughed. "I'm sure you will."

She put the book by her chair in the living room and grabbed the garage door opener and her keys from the kitchen counter on the way out the door. "You're driving."

I raised an eyebrow. I knew Dot still drove, but it honestly hadn't even occurred to me that she would be the one to drive us anywhere. "I assumed."

"What's wrong with my driving? I drive to the hospital every day, you know." There was that twinkle in her eye again.

I imagined Dot behind the wheel. She was in great shape, but the idea of an eighty-nine-year-old woman cruising down the freeways around Phoenix . . . I decided to let discretion be the better part of valor and changed the subject. "Where do you want to go?"

"Let's go back to Gallagher's. Those little burgers were really good."

Gallagher's was a sports bar about two miles from Dot's house; it's where we'd had lunch the previous week.

I opened the passenger door for her.

"I don't need your help. I'm old. I'm not infirm." The laughter in her voice told me that rather than being offended, Dot simply enjoyed yanking my chain.

"I can see that." I left her to her own devices.

The restaurant was practically empty, as it had been the previous week. Dot selected the same booth we'd sat in last time. It was becoming clear to me that Dot was a person who liked routine.

I ordered the Cobb salad and a Diet Coke. She ordered the sliders, or mini burgers, as she called them, the sweet potato fries, and a tall glass of water with lemon that I determined, based on observation, she likely wouldn't drink.

"You really should have some of that," I said, pointing at the glass.

"I hate drinking water."

"You live in Phoenix. You have to stay hydrated."

"I've lived here all my life. It doesn't bother me."

"You've spent your entire life in Phoenix?"

"I was born in my parents' farmhouse less than five miles from here. Never left, never wanted to."

Our food arrived.

"Are you going to eat all that?" She pointed her fork at my heaping bowl of salad.

"You bet."

She eyed my five-foot-one-inch frame speculatively. "Where are you going to put it all?"

I laughed. "I'll surprise you."

We briefly ate in silence. "How's Ricki?" I finally ventured.

Dot shook her head. "It's no good. She's in a lot of pain."

"I'm so sorry, Dot."

"We've been together forty-seven years. It'll be forty-eight years in October. I hoped we'd make it to fifty." Her voice trailed off. She glanced up at me. "I told her about your book. She couldn't believe I'd read it."

"Why?"

"Ricki's the reader. I haven't picked up a book in all the time we've been together."

"Seriously?"

Dot shrugged. "I never had time to read. I was always out playing ball or working. By the time we'd get home, I was too tired to do anything but put my feet up."

I digested this piece of information. "Why'd you read my book?"

"I read the back. It sounded interesting. I've never read anything like it. You wrote about people like me. My friends."

"You mean you'd never read anything with lesbian characters?"

"Yeah. I didn't know anyone wrote about things like that."

I was intrigued by this piece of information and by the fact that Dot was willing to talk to me openly about her sexuality and her relationship with Ricki. In my experience writing historical fiction, I'd had a very hard time getting people of Dot's generation to admit to same-sex relationships and to discuss what their lives had been like in the 1930s, '40s, and '50s.

"You said you and Ricki have been together forty-seven years. . . ." I hoped by leaving the comment open-ended, Dot would pick up the thread.

"She came over here after the 1962 season. She left her own team, the Orange [California] Lionettes, and her life on the west coast, to come here for me. Can you imagine that?" Dot looked at me, obviously perplexed. "Why would she do that?"

"Love?"

"She had a good job as a technical illustrator at Hughes Aircraft. She had a stake in the Lionettes. She had an apartment. She walked away from all of that." Dot speared a sweet potato fry, dipped it in ketchup, and popped it in her mouth.

"She fell in love with you, and she obviously knew you'd never leave Phoenix."

"No," Dot shook her head, "I never would've done what she did. I was a Rambler for life."

"So, Ricki played for the Ramblers after she got here?"

"Oh, yes. She helped me manage the team."

"Ford wasn't managing the team then?"

"No. He stepped away in the mid-1950s and left me in charge."

"Had Ricki lined up a job here before she moved?" I captured the last piece of hard-boiled egg on my fork and dipped it in the honey mustard dressing.

"No. Everything she looked at paid so much less than what she'd been making in California."

"So what did you do?"

"At first, we looked into buying a flower shop, or any kind of shop, really. To sell clothing or footwear, anything we could get into. We had about $2,500 each in cash. But we couldn't find what we were looking for.

"I'd been working in real estate with Ford since the 1940s. I started as his office manager. He taught me everything about the business. Eventually, I got my real estate license, and we bought a lot of properties together. We'd sell these low-cost mortgages for homes that weren't in great shape to folks who couldn't afford to buy homes otherwise. We held the paper on the houses. One day, Ricki said, 'You've got all these run-down houses. Why don't we try to fix up one of those ourselves and sell it?' So we did.

"Initially, we hired an older handyman Ford and I had worked with. He offered to teach us how to do things for ourselves. He taught us everything we needed to know. Ricki and I learned how to install and update plumbing and roofing and how to do electrical work, paint . . . the works."

"You were flipping houses in the 1960s, long before flipping houses was a thing."

"That's right. At one time, we had fifty houses here in Phoenix. I could drive you through the neighborhoods and point out every one. Of course, downtown didn't look then like it does now. It was the Wild West."

"That's amazing, Dot. Two women, in business for themselves with no men around. How did people respond to that?"

"Ricki and I were business partners. We had a partnership in every way and the papers to go with it. So if anyone questioned us, they could see that we were a business. If anyone had a problem with it, they never told us about it. We get people all the time who come up to us and say, 'You put us in such-and-such a property. We still live there.' And we remember every one of them."

I could see the pride Dot took in what she and Ricki had built. At a time when most unmarried women were being pushed into secretarial,

Ricki renovating one of the houses she and Dot flipped, circa 1970s.
Courtesy of the Dot Wilkinson Collection

teaching, or administrative positions, Dot and Ricki had made their way in the world through business acumen and hard physical labor. I told her as much.

"I never knew how much money we had. Ricki took care of that. She always wanted the security of having money in the bank. In the end, we made more than a million dollars. But I never knew that. I'd say, 'How much do we have?' Ricki wouldn't tell me, except to say that we had enough not to worry about being OK. But we were very frugal. We put away every penny."

"You should be very proud of what you two accomplished."

At my urging, Dot took a sip of lemon water. "I still don't know how we did it. We would drag ourselves home at night, every muscle aching."

"It was hard work," I said.

"Yeah. We had some really good times, some bad times, and lots of adventures, that's for sure."

Lunch ended, and I dropped Dot off. As I drove away, I thought about all that she and Ricki had done and accomplished together, both on and off the field. And I'd barely begun to scratch the surface.

4

Ricki Home, *A League of Our Own*, Thanksgiving Day

RICKI CAME HOME FROM THE HOSPITAL for the last time on August 28, 2010. Within a week, hospice had set up a hospital bed in Dot and Ricki's living room, and Dot was spending most of her time at Ricki's bedside. Ricki's niece, Chrissy, who was a nurse, came to stay and help, and another local nurse friend also became a regular fixture in the home.

I didn't see much of Dot in the next few weeks, so I was surprised when she called one day and told me she'd like me to come over and meet Ricki.

When I arrived, Ricki was lying in bed and Dot was sitting on the side of the bed, holding her hand. She beckoned me over.

"Lynn, this is my Ricki. Ricki, this is my friend, Lynn."

"Nice to meet you, Ricki."

"I've heard a lot about you."

I arched an eyebrow. "None of it good, I'm sure," I joked.

"Dottie tells me you remind her of me—lots of spunk and spitfire."

Dot had told me the same thing, but I found myself surprised that she'd shared this with Ricki.

"Beyond that, I can't believe you got her to read a book. In almost fifty years, I haven't been able to get her to sit down and read a book."

"Dot said as much. I didn't believe her."

"It's the truth."

We visited for a few more minutes. It was obvious that Ricki didn't have the stamina for much company. I said my goodbyes and went on my way.

I checked in with Dot at least once a week to see how she and Ricki were doing. I didn't want to intrude, but I also wanted to be supportive during such a difficult time.

In early October, Dot called with an invitation: "I wanted to know if you'd join me at the *League of Our Own* luncheon?"

"The what?" I was well familiar with the 1992 hit movie *A League of Their Own*, but Dot had told me early on that she hadn't been the catcher, Dottie, from the movie (played by Geena Davis), despite the fact that everyone thought she was.

"My good friend, Rose Mofford, a few others, and I started this organization many years ago. Once a year here in Phoenix, we hold a luncheon for all the old ballplayers from the teams around this area—the Ramblers, the Queens, the Sun City Saints. . . . It's the first Saturday in November."

"Rose Mofford? As in, the former governor of Arizona? That Rose Mofford?"

"Yeah. She's one of my oldest friends. She played for the A-1 Queens in 1939, long before she ever thought of politics."

"No kidding."

"So, will you come?"

"Of course. I'd be honored."

• • • • • • •

Saturday, November 6, 2010, was a typical sunny Phoenix day. Dot had told me to arrive a little early so she could introduce me around. When I entered the banquet facility at eleven o'clock, fully half an hour before the designated start to the event, gaggles of middle-aged and older women milled around chatting like old friends do. I checked in, printed my name on an adhesive tag, and stuck it to my blouse.

Long tables covered with tablecloths and filled to overflowing with scrapbooks, picture boards, and memorabilia lined the room. Attendees were looking through them, talking, laughing, and catching up. A dozen or more round tables of eight, set for lunch, took up the center of the space. A podium and microphone stood at the front of the room flanked by two head tables.

Dot was holding court at one of the head tables. We made eye contact and she got up and approached me.

"I want you to meet some people. First, we'd better get you a seat." She dragged me by the hand over to the table closest to the front. "Put your stuff here. You'll sit with Billie, Dobbie, Shirley, and Sis."

Apart from Billie, I recognized the remaining names from Ramblers newspaper clippings: first baseman Virginia "Dobbie" Dobson and third baseman/shortstop Shirley (Judd) Wade played on the Ramblers' 1948 and '49 world championship teams. The legendary home-run hitter Sis King and Billie joined the team in the 1950s.

I wanted to pinch myself. Here was softball royalty—the history of the heyday of women's ball.

"Come here." I blinked as Dot linked her arm through mine and carted me up to the front of the room. "Meet my friend, Rose."

There she was, larger than life. The state's first female governor, with her signature beehive hairdo and false eyelashes, gesticulated wildly and laughed uproariously at her own joke, told to a group gathered around her.

"Rosie, I want you to meet my good friend, Lynn."

"Hiya, kid."

"It's a pleasure to meet you."

"Any friend of Dottie's is a friend of mine." She clapped her arm around my shoulder and instructed someone to take a picture of us. Once a politician, always a politician.

The salads were served, followed by a solid plate of prime rib, mashed potatoes, and vegetables, chased by coffee and cheesecake. The conversation was lively as these longtime friends caught up on life. Once the tables were cleared, Rose and Dot got up in turn. Rose held forth on the history, longevity, and health of the organization. Dot got a laugh when she followed Rose with a joke about the rare peaceful gathering of Ramblers and Queens at the same event. These remarks were followed by updates from the heads of the Arizona Softball Hall of Fame and several other speakers and the raffling off of prizes brought by the attendees. Eventually, folks ran out of words and said heartfelt goodbyes until the next year, when they would gather again.

Many of the women stopped for a word with Dot, each of them expressing how much they missed seeing Ricki at the luncheon and instructing her to give Ricki a hug from them. I helped Dot load her scrapbooks and other memorabilia into her car and thanked her again for inviting me.

• • • • • • •

My time was occupied with a full schedule of book appearances for *Eyes on the Stars*, even as I was staring down a book deadline for my next novel. When I wasn't on the road, I was spending long days and nights wrestling with plot twists.

Dot and I spoke regularly as Ricki continued to deteriorate. About ten days after the softball luncheon, Dot called with an unexpected question.

"What are you doing for Thanksgiving?"

"Me?" The question caught me off guard. No one in my family had asked me my plans, and I'd resigned myself to spending a depressing holiday alone with a rotisserie chicken, green beans, and homemade brownies, as I'd done for several years.

"Yes, you. Every year, Ricki and I put on Thanksgiving for our close friends. Come."

"Me?" I knew I sounded dumb, but the invitation was so out of left field. Shouldn't I take time to consider?

"It's just a dozen or so of us who've been doing this for years. Billie will be there. Think about it. I don't need an answer today."

My stomach did a flip. Despite appearances to the contrary, at my core I was terminally shy and uncomfortable in social situations where I didn't know many people; this instance absolutely fit that description.

As a child, I would hide behind my mother and wrap myself around her knees whenever anyone approached and appeared to be paying attention to me. As an adult, I was only situationally extroverted, and then, most often when I was working.

Still, why shouldn't I go? It wasn't as though I had anyplace else to be. Surely in this case I could overcome my reluctance, couldn't I? After all, this was just a gathering of Dot and Ricki's friends, right?

"Yes. . . . Yes," I said, more firmly.

"Great."

"What can I bring? How about a dessert?" I didn't cook, but I baked killer chocolate chip cookies, and I could always buy a pie.

"Sold. Also, a bunch of us go out to lunch the day before. You should come to that too. Kay and Jo will be in from California. You should meet them."

"Kay and Jo?"

"Yeah. Kay Rich from Fresno and Joanne McLachlan, who played for Orange. They've been coming to Thanksgiving with us for years." Dot said the names like I should know who they were.

I had homework to do.

- - - - - - -

By the time I drove into the parking lot of the buffet-style restaurant where Dot told me to meet them, I was well-schooled on the original Western States Girls Major Softball League. It was formed in 1946 with original teams including the Ramblers, the Salt Lake City Shamrocks, the Lind and Pomeroy (Portland) Florists (later the Erv Lind Florists), and the Buena Park Lynx. In 1951, the league was renamed the Pacific Coast League, and the Orange Lionettes, the Fresno Rockets, the Huntington Park Blues, and Whittier Gold Sox were added, among others.

Kay Rich, who in 1963 was just the sixth woman to be inducted into the National Softball Hall of Fame, was widely hailed as the greatest athlete ever to play softball. She ruled the field at first base and shortstop for the Fresno Rockets for fourteen years, from the mid-1940s to the late 1950s. Jo McLachlan won national championships with the Orange Lionettes in the early 1950s. More softball royalty to add to my growing stable of legendary friends.

Lunch was a raucous affair, with two dozen ex-ballplayers all reminiscing and laughing together like one big family. I sat next to Dot and across the table from Kay. She was tall and rangy with the largest feet I'd ever seen on a woman, size twelves at least. I teased her about it, and she gave as good as she got. She was humble and quiet-spoken. I discovered that she'd been an educator—a physical education teacher—for her entire career.

Dot leaned in and joined the conversation. "Of all the players I played against, Kay was the one I respected more than any other. She was tough as nails but always fair and played the game right. Best player I ever played against."

I could've sworn I saw Kay blush. "Yeah, well, right back at you," she answered. "Not a better catcher in the game than Dottie."

"I never knew you felt that way at the time," Dot said. She turned to me. "We were competitors. We always respected each other, but we didn't become good friends until later."

I tucked this piece of information away, knowing I'd be asking Dot a lot more about this part of her history. I was sure of one thing when lunch ended: I liked Kay very much and was looking forward to talking more with her and Jo over Thanksgiving dinner.

On the way home from lunch, I stopped and bought a massive apple pie. That night, Thanksgiving Eve, I baked brownies and a double batch of chocolate chip cookies.

Dot said dinner would be at three o'clock, but I should arrive around one.

• • • • • • •

I arrived exactly at 1:00 PM on November 25. There were several cars in the driveway I didn't recognize. Apart from Kay and Jo, whom I'd lunched with the previous day, and my friend Billie, I was about to meet the rest of the gang whom Dot considered her family of choice. This group had been sharing Thanksgiving together for many years. I was the rookie. I had no idea what to expect.

I passed through the garage and entered the kitchen via the side door, as I normally did, my arms laden with desserts. The first thing I noticed was the smell—that delicious aroma of a turkey cooking in the oven. Next, I heard the sounds of conversation and laughter, old buddies good-naturedly teasing one another.

"Don't be bashful. Come on in."

I heard Dot's voice before I saw her. I peeked around the door. Dot stood next to the oven, turkey baster in hand.

"It smells great." I kissed her hello and maneuvered the desserts onto the already crowded kitchen counter as instructed.

"Ricki and I have been making Thanksgiving dinner for this bunch for over twenty years." Dot motioned me to follow her to the living room. She introduced me around as her "author friend." Then, before I even had a chance to catch everyone's name, she dragged me into the sunroom to see the table. It was beautifully set for twelve, with a centerpiece of seasonal flowers.

"As you can see, nothing fancy. We're just a group of friends who've become family over the years."

We rejoined the group, and I tried to fade into the background. I always was more comfortable observing than participating. But Dot's family members of choice were having none of it. Several of them grilled me about how I'd met Dot, where I was from, and a host of other questions. I found it interesting that some of them appeared to be leery of me, as if trying to suss out whether I had some ulterior motive for befriending Dot.

I sneaked a peek at Ricki, lying in her hospital bed in the middle of the living room, trying to follow strands of conversation. Although she put on a brave face, it was obvious that the noise and hubbub were too much for her.

At 3:00 PM, dinner was served. Dot sat at the head of the table and commanded that I sit next to her, to her right. The space on the other side of her was empty of a chair. Everyone hoped that Ricki would join us in her wheelchair. She did, briefly, but ate nothing, tired quickly, and retreated to bed. This was to be her last Thanksgiving, even as it proved to be my first of many with this gang.

Whatever my previous experiences had been of tense family holiday gatherings, that first Thanksgiving at Dot's and every one thereafter were filled with easy camaraderie, love, good-natured teasing, excellent and plentiful food, and fun.

5

Ricki's Death and the
Next Chapter

Between Thanksgiving and Christmas 2010, Dot and I kept in touch weekly via telephone. Ricki's health was failing rapidly. The sadness in Dot's voice hurt my heart.

In between these conversations, I was receiving more detailed updates from Billie. She and I were meeting regularly for brunch at an IHOP near her home as I interviewed her about her life and career as the first Black woman to break the color barrier in major league softball.

I paid Dot and Ricki a visit shortly before Christmas and again just after the new year. On that last occasion, I found myself momentarily alone with Ricki. I stood over the bed so that she could see me clearly. She reached out and took my hand, gripping it firmly.

Although we exchanged not a single word, her eyes conveyed the message with crystal clarity. Ricki was asking me to watch over Dot—to keep her engaged in the world when she could no longer be here to do so herself. She was passing me the baton.

I squeezed her hand in what I hoped was a gesture of reassurance. It was a promise I intended to keep.

• • • • • • •

On January 10, 2011, I sat across the table from Billie at IHOP. "Ricki passed."

"When?"

"Yesterday. The funeral is Saturday. It would mean a lot to Dot if you could be there."

My heart sank. I was leaving Saturday morning for Dallas for a book appearance. There was no way I could cancel the appearance on such short notice. "I-I can't." I tried to explain.

In her typically low-key way, Billie said nothing. She didn't have to—we both knew I should be at the funeral. I was miserable.

After I left Billie, I picked up a sympathy card and spent some time gathering my thoughts. Dot and Ricki had spent the past forty-eight years together. What could I say that would help ease Dot's pain? What could anyone say? I wrote from the heart and hoped my words would bring Dot comfort, addressed the envelope, and stuck the card in the mail.

The next day, I picked up a copy of the *Arizona Republic* and searched the pages for Ricki's obituary. I found it on page B6 with the other obituaries:

> *Caito, Ricki*
>
> *Born: Sept. 14, 1925 in Oakland, CA. Ricki was preceeded [sic] by her parents Mary and Robert Caito and Brother George De Ponte. Ricki is survived by her long time [sic] companion Dot Wilkinson, her dog Desi . . .*

I made a donation in Ricki's name to Hospice of the Valley, which was one of the designated organizations listed in the obit. I wanted to call Dot, but I imagined she was busy with company, making final arrangements, and the myriad other things that go along with end-of-life issues. I didn't want to insert myself at such a difficult moment. I would get in touch as soon as I returned from Dallas the following Wednesday.

. . . .

I picked up Dot for our lunch date at 11:30 AM on Thursday. The house seemed so empty and quiet. As always, Desi, Dot and Ricki's bichon frise, greeted me at the door by bouncing off my shin. I petted her briefly.

"I'm sorry I missed the service." Dot gave me her usual kiss, and I enveloped her in a long hug.

"It was beautiful. Lots of people got up and spoke. Did you see the obituary?" Dot pulled me into the sunroom, where she had the newspaper folded open to the page with Ricki's picture and write-up. "That's my favorite picture of her."

The picture was of Ricki standing in the on-deck circle, waiting to come up to bat. She wore the satin shorts and jersey top of her beloved Orange Lionettes. She had eye black under her eyes and two bats slung over her right shoulder. The shot must've been taken in the late 1950s.

Dot's fingers rested on the image. "Now there was a ballplayer." She smiled wanly up at me.

"Yep."

"Did you see that I put right in there, '. . . survived by her longtime companion, Dot Wilkinson'?"

"I did."

"I don't care that people can see that. That's what she was to me. If people have a problem with that, too bad."

I blinked. "Dot? Why would anyone have a problem with you and Ricki? Everyone already knew you were together, right?"

"What? Of course not."

"You lived together for forty-eight years, Dot. What did people think was going on?"

She shrugged. "We just never talked about it."

"Are you telling me you came out as a lesbian in Ricki's obituary?"

"Yep." She seemed rather pleased with herself. "I'd be damned if I was going to bury her without everyone knowing what she was to me."

Estelle "Ricki" Caito in the on-deck circle for the Orange Lionettes circa 1958. *Courtesy of the Dot Wilkinson Collection*

I knew my jaw must have been hanging open. I couldn't help it. Dot never had hidden her sexuality from me. I assumed it had been thus with everyone in her life. I said as much.

"A bunch of the kids were here with Ricki and me recently—my great-nieces and nephews and great-greats too. Missy, Lisa, Ralph—I don't remember who all was here. I just sat them down and told them how it was."

"How did they react?"

"They told me they already figured it out, had known it for years, and that they loved Ricki like an aunt. They just never said anything. Shocked me. I didn't realize they knew."

"That's awesome that they were so nonchalant about it."

"Yeah." We were silent for a minute. "You hungry?"

"You bet."

"Let's get out of here." She paused in the hallway, pointed to one of the many pictures on the wall, and ran her fingers over the image. "This was the last picture taken of her. Doesn't she look beautiful?"

The snapshot was of Ricki lying in the hospital bed in the living room, the same hospital bed that still stood in the center of the living room, now empty and stripped of bedding. She was smiling at the camera.

"She sure does."

We went to Gallagher's. By now, we had a designated booth at the joint. This would remain true for nearly a decade's worth of weekly lunches. I ordered my customary Cobb salad with honey mustard dressing, and Dot ordered her sliders with sweet potato fries.

We talked for a long time.

Dot's many talents did not extend to playing the tuba. In fact, the only musical instrument she ever played was the piano—and that only briefly. She posits that she most likely "borrowed" the dented tuba in this photo from her older brother, Bill. *Courtesy of the Dot Wilkinson Collection*

Part Two

SPRING
TRAINING

6

Dot: On Her Own for the Very First Time

ON ONE OF OUR FIRST VISITS after Ricki's death, Dot made an extraordinary admission to me: "This is the first time in my entire life I've ever lived alone."

"Dot, you're eighty-nine years old. You mean to tell me, in all that time, you've never been on your own?"

"Never. I was born at home. From the moment I took my first breath, I lived at home or my folks lived with me. That was true for their entire lives."

"Even when you were in relationships?"

"Even then. When my dad died in 1958, my folks were living in an in-law apartment on the property on St. Charles Street that my girlfriend at the time, Kay, and I bought and lived in together. She and my brother-in-law, Joe, built that separate apartment out behind the house for my parents. When my mom died in 1973, she still was living with me and Ricki on St. Charles Street."

"And after that?"

"A few years later, Ricki and I found this house, and we've lived here ever since."

I tried to fathom that in nearly nine decades, Dot had never, ever, lived by herself.

Where once I thought the story of Dot was all about softball, now I found myself even more curious about Dot's upbringing, her parents and family life.

7

Dot's Parents' Journey

As fate would have it, I didn't have to wait long to get some answers. It started with a random question from Dot.

"Do you know how to look up somebody's family?" she asked.

"You mean, to do genealogical research, like where your family came from?"

"Yeah."

"I do. You can look it up on your computer."

"I don't have a computer."

I blinked. "You don't . . ." My voice trailed off.

"I don't need one of those things. Heck, I don't even have a credit card."

"You don't . . ." I was beginning to repeat myself.

"Nope. Never wanted one. I pay for everything with either cash or a check."

I shook my head. "Unbelievable. What do you need to know about your family?"

"Well, my mother was an Austen. I know that, somehow, we're related to the famous writer, Jane Austen, but I don't know how. Can you figure that out for me?"

"I can try. Tell me more about your mom and family and I'll see if I can find out anything."

In the end, I never was able to trace the family connection to Jane Austen, although based on her ancestors' geographic history, I agree with Dot that there is one. What I uncovered instead was the fascinating tale of the Austen/Wilkinson migration from England to Phoenix and what happened in the decades that followed.

· · · · · · ·

Allan and Alice Wilkinson's home in Middlesex, England, circa 1906. *Courtesy of the Dot Wilkinson Collection*

By the time Dorothy Elsie Wilkinson came along on October 9, 1921, her parents, Allan and Alice (Austen) Wilkinson, were well-established on the ten-acre farm on Seventh Avenue between Highland Road and East Roeser Road in Phoenix, Arizona. They had arrived from their native England nine years earlier with their three-year-old daughter Joan.

Alice gave birth to a son, Bill, in 1915, and a daughter, Ruth, in 1917, at home. Dot, who also was born at home, was the last of the Wilkinson children.

Life on the farm was a far cry from Allan and Alice's comfortable, middle-class existence in Middlesex, on the outskirts of London. Back home, a couple of Allan's eleven siblings carried on the successful gold wedding ring manufacturing business established by Allan's grandfather, John, in 1832. Allan had no interest in partaking in the family business.

Alice's parents, who were well enough off that Alice had never learned to cook or make a fire herself in their native England, her sister Ina, and brother Harry, had crossed the pond in 1906 to seek Arizona's climate for Harry's health. That combination of factors enticed Allan and Alice to pack up and leave their upscale London home.

When Allan and Alice relocated and took up farming, they started from scratch. Allan and his brother-in-law, Harry, built the Wilkinson homestead on one or two of the ten acres bordered by a ditch that ran the length of the property in front of the house. The house was wood framed and screened in, with wooden floors, a large great room, and a series of small bedrooms that were separated by flimsy cloth dividers. The bedrooms were freezing cold in the winter and boiling hot in the summer.

Although the house had electricity and an icebox, it had no running water, a constant source of embarrassment to Dot as soon as she was old enough to go to school and discovered that all her friends and classmates had indoor plumbing and toilets. A well pump in the backyard provided water for the house, and Alice heated the water in galvanized tubs over the large potbellied wood stove to prepare the children's baths. Allan built an outhouse, and pages torn from the Sears, Roebuck and Company catalog served as toilet paper.

Alice Wilkinson with her children, Bill and Joan, in front of the family farm in Phoenix, circa 1918. *Courtesy of the Dot Wilkinson Collection*

At the outset, Alice would ride into town via unpaved lanes in a horse-drawn carriage led by her spirited horse, Pink Lady. Young Joan and Bill rode alongside her. It was the same route the Navajo traders traveled to ferry their goods into town. Eventually, the family purchased a car, making the journey easier.

Allan learned how to plant various crops and fruit trees and to raise cows and chickens to sustain the family. He sold corn, alfalfa, and cotton he'd grown and Alice had picked, often dragging infant Dot along behind her in a cotton sack.

When Dot was old enough, she milked the cows, a chore she didn't mind, since her mother used some of the fresh cream and fruit from the peach and pear trees to make homemade ice cream for the family every day.

At various times, Allan took odd jobs. He worked at Roeser's, a general store not far from the house, and once headed up north for a three-week stint to help a family friend prospect for gold.

Allan also brewed his own beer in the family cellar, a source of contention with Dot's mother, who didn't drink and chafed that her husband liked his drink a little too much.

On Sundays, Allan would take the family for a drive, and Alice would cook a roast with potatoes and vegetables over the woodstove. During the summers, when the heat was unbearable in the house, Dot and her siblings would soak their bed sheets in the ditch, lay the sheets down on the earth, and sleep outside under the stars. In the chilly desert winters, with the cold and wind blasting in through the wood-framed structure, they would pile extra blankets on the beds.

The life was simple, rudimentary, and hard, but the family never went hungry.

When she was school-aged, Dot, in her one hand-me-down skirt and blouse, would walk partway to Roosevelt Grammar School, then would meet up with her friend John, who lived a quarter of a mile away, and together they would roller-skate on the paved roads the rest of the nearly

Alice Wilkinson with her children, Bill and Joan, on the way to town from the farm, circa 1916. *Courtesy of the Dot Wilkinson Collection*

four-mile journey. It was a carefree time of shooting marbles after school (Dot would lose, and John would win them back for her), picking and eating fresh fruit from the trees, swimming in the ditch in front of the Wilkinson farm or in the canal on Baseline Road, and playing speedball (which was invented the year Dot was born and combines skills from soccer, basketball, and football) in the mornings before school and various sports in gym class.

8

Dot & Babe

ONE DAY, DOT'S DAD piled her into the family Chevy and drove her down to Twenty-Fourth Street and Van Buren. He'd heard about a horse for sale, and he wanted to get it for Dot. Dot adored horses. With Babe, it was love at first sight. Dot's father gave her a boost up onto the horse's bare back, she took hold of the bridle's reins, and she rode her new friend all the way home as her dad drove along beside them in the car.

For years, Dot and some boy neighbors would spend long, lazy afternoons riding their steeds on the dirt roads along the canal. Today, those roads are some of the busiest thoroughfares in downtown Phoenix.

Babe wasn't the only horse on the farm; Dot's father kept two large workhorses. Often, she would accompany her father as he used the horses to harrow the fields. Dot's parents admonished her that these horses were not family pets. She was not to try to ride them—they were not like Babe.

Ever headstrong, one afternoon, eight-year-old Dot wandered down to the fenced-in field where those horses were grazing. She'd made up her mind to ride one of those behemoths. As she reached under the fence, the horse pawed her right arm. Bleeding and with the skin of her forearm

Dot's horse, Babe. Her father purchased her the mare for $10, and Dot rode her bareback all the way home, with her father driving next to them in the family car. *Courtesy of the Dot Wilkinson Collection*

ripped nearly off, Dot went in search of her mother and her sister Ruth, who were making ice cream in the front yard.

"I knew I wasn't supposed to be doing what I was doing, so I lied and told my mom and Ruth that I'd been trying to feed the horse and he pawed me. I must've looked horrible, because before I knew what was happening, they hustled me over to the next-door neighbor's house.

"Mrs. Hershey was a nurse. She bandaged me up, and Mother and Ruth took me over to my father. He was working at the Roeser Grocery Store at the corner of Roeser Road and Central Avenue. He put me in the car and took me to the doctor. A big hunk of meat [presumably muscle, tendons, etc.] had come out. They stitched it all back in and sent me on my way.

"Well, within a month it all went rotten. The doctor wanted to amputate my arm. He insisted that was the only way. My father told him, 'Oh no, you're not going to do that.' That's what I heard my dad say. He said,

'You can't do that.' And he wouldn't let him. Thank God! I wouldn't have had that good right arm.

"Finally, when the doctor realized my father wasn't going to budge, he cleaned it out as best he could and sewed me back together again. My dad took me to the doctor every day for thirty days after that. They cleaned and dressed my forearm every single day."

Dot rolled up her sleeve to show me. "See that scar? It's still there. Reminds me every day how lucky I was that my dad was as stubborn as I am."

I think about how different Dot's life would've been if not for her father's persistence. Lucky, indeed.

· · · · · · ·

"Your poor mother had her hands full with you."

Dot had that twinkle in her eye, the one I'd come to recognize meant, "You've got no idea." I looked forward to these moments, because I knew another good story was sure to follow.

"Well, Mother had it in her head that I should learn an instrument. She was teaching my older sister, Ruth, to play the piano, so Mother set me to learning the piano too. One day, I was supposed to be practicing on the piano. But I was messing around, and I fell off the piano stool and into the glass. We had glass doors there and my mother came, and I was catching hell, and Ruth says, 'Mom, you better check. There's a lot of blood.' And I had fallen through and I don't know whether I'd cut my face or something. Now I was bleeding, so she took me and fixed me up. I said, 'No more practice.'"

"I assume your mother agreed to that."

Dot sat up a little straighter, proud of herself. "I never played that piano again."

"This was before you started playing softball, right? What did you do to occupy your time instead?"

"I played outside with some of the neighborhood kids. The Reeves boys lived up the road and around the corner. I used to go over there.

We'd play, and sometimes we rode horses together." Dot then got a far-away look on her face. "Except this one day, it must've been before we started riding. They had a crazy uncle who lived with them. He used to talk to me all the time. I was out there by myself, and he threw me down in a ditch and jumped on top of me."

My eyes got wide. "What did you do?"

"Mr. Reeves, my friends' father, came along, and I guess he saw the uncle and he probably knew how he was. So, he just grabbed a hold of him and threw him across the road."

The thought of young Dot narrowly avoiding a sexual assault left me cold. "You must've been scared out of your mind."

Dot shrugged. "I probably should've been, but I wasn't. He was still around a long time after. He never bothered me again."

"Did you tell your parents?"

Dot shrugged again, as if what happened was no big deal. "Probably not." And she was on to the next topic. In this case, the subject was sports other than softball and bowling that Dot took up in her youth.

"I remember that the Roeser Grocery Store, where my dad worked, had a tennis court on the side of it. My parents used to play there on Sunday mornings, and they'd take me along. Sometimes they'd sit me in an apple crate to watch.

"I went there when I was very young, because I remember my parents used to leave me with a lady that lived in an apartment with the Roesers. . . . She was an artist, and she used to take me over there and dress me up and then draw pictures of me."

"How old were you then?"

"I don't know. I was maybe five or six years old."

Those early years run together for Dot, and I quickly learned that asking her to pinpoint dates was an exercise in futility.

She continued her story as if I hadn't interrupted her. "Spending those Sunday mornings watching my parents play tennis is how I knew how to keep score and do all that. When I went to high school, I already knew how to play tennis.

"I can't remember when I first played, but I know when I started high school, my mother gave me her racket. So, I showed up with her racket, and the tennis coach, a woman named Lorette Cooper, whom I had a crush on, said to me, 'You can't play with that racket. You need a better one.'

"I asked her how much it cost. She said it cost nine dollars [the equivalent of $197 today]. I told her I didn't know if my parents could afford to get me a new racket. They didn't have any money. Still, somehow they found a way because they got me one. I don't know how they did it.

"Once I had the racket, Coach Cooper told me, 'Go out there and hit balls against the wall.' Our tennis court backed up to the auditorium and it was a big, tall auditorium and we could hit balls against the wall. That was Phoenix [Union] High School.

Dot learned to keep score by watching her parents play tennis on Sunday mornings on the court next to the Roeser Grocery Store.
Courtesy of the Dot Wilkinson Collection

"So, I finally told her . . . I said, 'I know how to play tennis. Can I please quit? I don't want to volley against a wall.'

"I finally . . . I took a ball and I hit it clear up on top of the roof. She said, 'Well, I guess you can play.' So, I started playing then and so I was on the tennis team all four years. We won a state championship. I was number one. Well, I was number two the first year, and then I was number one from then on."

• • • • • • •

The Phoenix Union High School tennis team, with Dot on the lower left. *Courtesy of the Dot Wilkinson Collection*

Dot, age fourteen, on one of her many summer days spent swimming and diving at the pool at University Park. *Courtesy of the Dot Wilkinson Collection*

"I was number one from then on. . . ." That became a familiar refrain in Dot's life when it came to sports.

Apart from speedball, horseback riding, and tennis, Dot spent much of her youth tagging along with her sister Ruth, who was four years Dot's senior.

"I was close to Ruth. She and her friend, Katie, used to thumb a ride to town every day to go to University Park, where they had a public swimming pool. I'd tag along. That was when you weren't afraid to go out and get a ride with anybody. And we'd come home that way after dark.

"They had a diving coach at University Park. There was a forty-foot diving platform, and I was at the age when you weren't afraid to flip and do one-and-a-half, two-and-a-half revolutions, or whatever. When I was fourteen, I won the diving championship."

Dot wasn't just a natural athlete; she was a gifted one, with a high degree of body awareness, control, and strength. She never had to work too hard at whatever sport she tried; she simply excelled at all of them.

It was that remarkable, innate ability that caught the eye of Ford Hoffman, a sixth-grade history teacher and coach at Roosevelt Grammar School.

The 1934 PBSW Ramblers: Top row, from left to right: Peggy Hoffman, Lillian Acuff, Norma Acuff, Mickey Sullivan, Maureen Patterson, June Griner, unknown, Jean Klont. Bottom row, from left to right: Dot Wilkinson, Florabell Beachum, Esther Holton, Louise Miller, Katie Gould Moore, Margaret Vance, unknown. *Courtesy of the Dot Wilkinson Collection*

Part Three

THE
NATURAL

9

Dot Finds a Mentor in Ford

Young Dot didn't care for school, didn't pay much attention, and didn't apply herself . . . until it came time for gym class and extracurricular sports. She particularly loved taking part in the Roosevelt Grammar School track meets.

The meets were the brainchild of the school's sixth-grade history teacher, Ford Hoffman. In many ways, Hoffman was ahead of his time. Although Dot's school was all-White, Coach Hoffman encouraged the young Black students who lived in the district and attended the school down the street to participate. He would drive the bus to collect those students and transport them to Roosevelt and home after the meets.

Hoffman also was a booster of girls in sports. So when ten-year-old Dot stepped up at a meet and set a record for distance at the baseball throw, he paid attention.

"He came up to me and said, 'How would you like to play on a softball team that someday goes to Chicago to play in the world championships?'

"I said, 'Where's Chicago?' I'd never been out of south Phoenix, so I had no concept what he was talking about. But I thought it sounded exciting, so I said, 'Sure.'"

That fortuitous encounter marked the beginning of what would be a lifelong mentorship and friendship between Dot and Ford Hoffman.

"Ford was a father figure to me. It's funny—it wasn't until he was gone that I really appreciated everything he did for me. I never realized. I wish I'd told him when he was alive.

"Anyway, in those early, early days, he'd be driving the Black kids home after a meet and he'd see me having fights in the street with some of the boys or getting into trouble. He'd stop the bus, open the door, and tell me to get on the bus. He'd make me stay on the bus until he'd dropped the last kid off, and then he'd drop me off.

"Pretty soon, he put together a team. His wife, Peggy, and my older sister, Ruth, played. He asked me to be the bat girl. That lasted about half a season, and before I knew it, he asked me to join the team. I was eleven years old. That was in 1933."

Hoffman named the team the Phoenix Ramblers and rounded up a benefactor. That sponsor was the Petersen, Brooke, Steiner, & Wist Supply and Equipment Company, formed a decade earlier by five World War I veterans who met as patients in Fort Whipple Veterans Hospital in Prescott, Arizona, shortly after the war ended.

Remarkably, that single school/equipment supply company sponsored the team from the moment of its inception until Dot and Ricki retired the PBSW Ramblers in 1965. Each year, the team would be supplied with two complete sets of uniforms, two sets of warm-ups, two pairs of cleats, and two gloves for each player, along with bats, balls, and catcher's equipment. In return, PBSW received advertising and publicity.

10

The Early Years of Softball

IN THOSE FIRST FEW FORMATIVE YEARS, Ford scrambled to find local competition for the Ramblers. Over the course of the summer months from 1933 to 1935, Ford and several associates cobbled together a Phoenix-area four-team, fast-pitch, all-amateur league. All games were played locally, and, according to Dot, the girls didn't practice much.

The official rules of softball were just being hashed out. The bases were to be sixty feet apart, the ball was to be white and twelve inches in circumference. The distance between the pitcher's mound and home plate was set at thirty-seven feet, eight-and-one-half inches. An official softball game was seven innings long.

Over the years, the rules would be changed multiple times. The distance between home plate and the pitcher's mound moved to forty feet, then forty-three, and finally back to thirty-eight feet in 1952. Bunting, which initially was forbidden, became legal in 1938. Spiked cleats, which also were initially taboo, were allowed beginning in 1936. The tenth player was eliminated in 1947.

Initially, Dot played second base for the Ramblers. When Ford picked up a second baseman from California in 1936 or '37, Dot moved to being the tenth fielder.

"Ford picked up a girl named Alberta 'Al' Berry from California. She played with us for a while. She was an infielder—a very good one—and a great hitter. So, because she played second base, Ford moved me to the tenth player. Back then, we had ten on the field. The tenth player could either play in the infield or in the outfield. I played wherever the coach wanted me to. I just wanted to play."

Dot returned to second base when Berry went back to California before the 1938 season got underway.

Although she was a natural right-hander, Ford taught Dot to bat left-handed.

"He said, 'You're not big enough to hit the ball. I'll teach you how to bunt, and you can run. And we'll do it from the left side.' That's why I never hit right-handed at all, ever. I wasn't a switch-hitter. I just hit left-handed. I tried hitting righty a few times, but I couldn't. I was no good at batting right-handed. I could place the ball pretty good where I wanted to from the left side."

In fact, Dot was quick, and hitting from the left side of home plate gave her an advantage getting to first base faster. Other than swinging a golf club later in life, batting was the only thing Dot ever did left-handed.

• • • • • • •

The mid-1930s proved consequential to Dot for myriad reasons. Dot's oldest sister, Joan, fourteen years Dot's senior, had moved away years earlier, married, and started a family of her own. Bill, the next oldest of the Wilkinson children, relocated several hours north to Flagstaff, where he married and set himself up running a service station.

Of most consequence to Dot, though, was the loss of the daily companionship of her beloved sister and best friend, Ruth.

On August 22, 1935, eighteen-year-old Ruth married her sweetheart, Joe Moore. Ruth quit the softball team and settled down into her own life. Although she and Dot remained close throughout their lives and Ruth and Joe were regular fixtures in the Wilkinson house, things simply weren't the same.

Then, in early 1936, a tragic accident spelled even more change for the Wilkinsons. Dot's beloved uncle, Harry Austen, owned a thirty-acre farm at Twenty-Eighth Street and Baseline. More than anyone else, he largely was responsible for helping establish his sister, Alice, and her husband, Allan, in Phoenix. On April 18, 1936, Harry was out in his fields, killing weeds using fire from a gasoline torch strapped to his back, when the equipment he was using malfunctioned. He suffered severe burns over most of his body and succumbed to his injuries four days later.

"Harry's was the first funeral I ever attended. I was fourteen years old. I remember that made an impression on me. His kids were close to my age, and we used to go to their house for Christmas and other holidays."

When Dot relayed these events and others like them, she never lingered long in the sad places, pivoting quickly back to happier subjects with, "Let's talk about something else, OK?"

In this case, that something else was her transition to high school, a new group of friends, the softball boom in Arizona and beyond, and the growing importance of softball in Dot's life.

11

The High School Years

ON THE HOME FRONT, Dot was busy adjusting to attending Phoenix Union High School. "When I went to high school, I just barely made it through all the time. I wasn't an A-1 student, I'll tell you, because I didn't do much studying. That's something I never worried too much about, the classroom.

"Only time was when I guess I was just starting in high school and I had to give a forty-five-minute speech on something and get up in front of the class and do it. I thought, *Oh my God.* So I picked tennis. I got by with that real good. I started out with the tennis rackets and all that kind of stuff and made my way through it and did all right, and after that, I wasn't afraid to talk. And I've been talking ever since."

It didn't help Dot much that the end of softball season ran over into the start of the school year. "We would leave in September to go to the national tournament, and then classes would have started by the time I got back. I missed stuff and I just thought, *Well, hell.* I didn't worry about it. Like, I took a typing class, and I never did learn. Every year I would miss the start of that class. I never did get it right. I finally taught myself how to type years later."

At Phoenix Union, Dot made quick friends with a group of six or seven girls. "We all started out playing sports together as freshmen, and we played all the way through."

Dot listed off the names: "Dorothy Filipi, Jean, Fern, Rachel, Rhea, Marge, and Eleanor Firpo. She was one of my best friends. We did a lot together." Dot got that faraway look as she got lost in the memories. "We called her the chicken plucker. She would always say, 'I have to go home and pluck chickens.' Her dad owned the big chicken place over there on Central Avenue.

"Firpo was a speedster. She was the fastest girl on the track team. I don't remember how it happened, but Firpo got picked to race against Babe Didrikson. I remember meeting her on the track where they held the exhibition race here in Phoenix. Of course, Firpo lost. She was a fast runner, but she wasn't in the same class as Didrikson."

"Babe Didrikson Zaharias?" I asked, dumbfounded. "As in the 1932 Olympic two-time gold medalist and professional golfer? The greatest female athlete ever?"

Dot bristled a little at this last part. She was never impressed by fame or accolades.

"Anyway, Firpo played for the Queens."

And, just like that, Dot circled back to softball, the nexus of her world.

• • • • • • •

In 1936 or '37, a men's softball player named Larry Walker created a rival women's team in Phoenix. He called them the Queens. His self-professed aim was to draw crowds with sex appeal in addition to excellence on the ball field. He vehemently denied, as one magazine at the time posited, that strenuous athletics were detrimental to femininity and that the best female athletes were somewhat masculine in appearance—which, naturally, was code for *lesbian.*

"We pass them up," Walker declared, in an oblique reference to these "masculine-type girls." "It is possible to be an athlete and maintain feminine charm." Walker outfitted the girls in short, satin skirts over brief tights. Queens players, according to Walker, were chosen "on the basis of character first, feminine charm second, and ability to play ball third. Our team is based on good-looking girls. Even though it is one of the top girls teams in the world, it could draw well if it won very few games."

Dot shared this quote and her thoughts about Larry Walker with a bitter laugh. He was far from her favorite person. "If only he knew how many of his players were gay." Then she shrugged, seemingly unbothered by the homophobic and sexist attitude. "That's just the way it was back then."

Over the years, the Queens had a variety of sponsors, but to the Ramblers and their fans, they forever would be simply the Queens. The intense rivalry between the two teams lasted for decades. Dot was friends with many of the Queens, but once they took the field, personal friendship counted for nothing.

The enmity extended far beyond the players to the fans as well. Loyalties were fierce. "If you were a Ramblers fan, you sat in the Ramblers section," Dot said. "If you were a Queens fan, you sat in the Queens section. You never fraternized with 'the enemy.' You wouldn't believe how many times a fight in the stands had to be broken up."

Ford, who continued to manage the all-amateur Ramblers simply for the love of the game and his players, set his sights on broadening interstate beyond just the Queens. He arranged contests between the Ramblers and a variety of West Coast teams, including a San Diego squad and one from Hollywood that featured a young movie star named Kay Rohrer, who years later would play a large role in Dot's life.

By 1937, when Dot was a sophomore in high school, the Ramblers had secured a place as a state and national amateur powerhouse, and Ford was ready to make good on his promise to take the Ramblers to the World Softball Championships in Chicago.

During the course of that regular season, the Ramblers accumulated a record of 33–1. On September 1 and 2, 1937, they clinched the Arizona state girls' softball title by trouncing a combination Tempe-Scottsdale team, 6–1 and 16–3, in the best-of-three series under the lights at University Park.

The next morning, the team boarded a bus for the three-day trip to Chicago. The World Softball Championships would open September 10, and the Ramblers would spend a week getting acclimated and practicing.

When Ford and the girls arrived at the towering Allerton Hotel at 701 North Michigan Avenue, they were exhausted. If Dot had been impressed by the remarkable view from the skyscraper, she didn't remember it. Nor did she recall any of the sights Ford arranged for them to see, though she was certain he did.

Dot cared about only one thing: playing and winning softball games. And so, when she found herself in that tunnel underneath Soldier Field with fifteen hundred other players, waiting for the opening ceremony to begin, Dot wasn't thinking about the pageantry or the pomp. She was itching to take that first swing.

The Ramblers took the field against the team from Council Bluffs, Iowa, that night under threatening skies. When the clouds finally burst open, the Ramblers were up, 6–0. The umpires postponed the game until the next day. The delay meant that, to reach the finals, the Ramblers first would have to win the postponed game and then the next two contests as well, all in one day.

The next morning, the girls finished off Council Bluffs, 7–2 on the strength of Bea Cline's and Al Berry's home runs. That afternoon, they would face the daunting task of trying to dispatch the previous year's world champion runners-up—the Montgomery V-Eights of Chicago.

Everyone picked the favored Chicago team to win . . . everyone, that is, except the Ramblers players and Ford Hoffman. The opposing pitcher, Boots Klupping, was averaging fifteen strikeouts per game, and the Chicago team had home-field advantage.

But what the Ramblers had that afternoon was a veteran ace pitcher, twenty-one-year-old Louise Miller, who was in top form. The Ramblers scratched across two runs in the second inning, and Miller took care of the rest. In the end, she hurled a no-hit gem, allowing only three walks and two other runners, both of whom reached base on fielding errors. No Chicago player got farther than first base.

Dot and her teammates barely had time to celebrate. They returned to the hotel after the game, took a short rest, grabbed something to eat, and headed back to the diamond, where they eliminated the Capper Girls of Topeka, Kansas, 4–1 in the nightcap.

That win catapulted the Ramblers into the semifinals. But achieving the semifinals in their first world championship appearance wasn't enough. Dot wanted to win it all. At fifteen, she already was a fierce competitor, accustomed to winning at whatever contest she entered. Second, third, or fourth best? That wasn't for her.

The Ramblers took the field against the Rayls Sport Shop Girls of Detroit in the semifinals on September 14, 1937. The weather was clear and cool—perfect for softball. But it didn't take long for the temperature on the field to rise.

In the top of the third inning, with a runner on second and two outs, Alma Miller, the Detroit center fielder, stroked a single into the outfield. Dot, playing rover, fielded the ball cleanly as the runner who'd been on second rounded third and tried to score.

Dot unleashed a strike to Ramblers catcher Norma Acuff in plenty of time. Acuff took the throw cleanly and blocked the plate neatly, fully expecting to tag out the incoming Detroit runner. Instead, the runner lowered her shoulder like a football player heading for the goal line and plowed into Acuff, forcing her to drop the ball. Detroit took a 1–0 lead.

In the bottom of the fifth inning, Dot figured in the action prominently again, as the Ramblers had a chance to tie the game. Left fielder Gladys Langford took off for home on Dot's short fly to right field. Langford was thrown out at the plate.

In the bottom of the sixth inning, the Ramblers came to bat still trailing by one run, with only six outs left to turn the game around. Third baseman Mickey Sullivan started things off with a single. First baseman Esther Holton reached on an error, allowing Sullivan to advance to second. Peggy Hoffman hit into a fielder's choice, resulting in Sullivan being put out at third for the first out. Five outs to go.

Gladys Langford worked out a walk, loading the bases for Al Berry, one of the Ramblers' best sluggers. Berry, a great contact hitter, launched a sharp ground ball that one of the Detroit fielders failed to handle. Holton bolted home, tying the game.

The scene was set. Dot came to bat with one out, the score knotted at one, and the bases loaded. Like Berry, Dot was a reliable contact hitter; she rarely struck out.

Most fifteen-year-old girls on such a pressure-packed world stage would've wilted. Dot wasn't that girl. She dug her metal cleats into the dirt, set her feet firmly, and glanced down to first, where Ford was standing in the coach's box.

"Make it count," he yelled to her, over the deafening noise of the crowd in the stands.

Dot saw the pitch well, shifted her hips to put her weight into the swing, and took her best cut. Unfortunately, she got under the ball, popping a high fly off the first baseline in foul territory.

Detroit catcher Olga Madar moved up the line and easily fielded Dot's fly ball for the second out of the inning, after which she threw the ball to the pitcher, who was standing in the box.* Then Madar stooped to pick up her catcher's mask, which she'd flung off in order to help her make the catch cleanly.

Amateur Softball Association (ASA) rules were clear: once the pitcher was in the box, ready to pitch, no runner could advance. In this case, there was only one problem: the catcher wasn't anywhere near home plate, leaving the pitcher with no one to whom to pitch.

Ford immediately assessed the situation and concluded that even if the pitcher possessed the ball, if there was no catcher behind the plate ready to receive a pitch, then the pitcher counted as a regular fielder, thus leaving the runner free to advance. He signaled Peggy to tag up at third and score, which she did. The umpire called her out for leaving third base

---

* For a period of time, Amateur Softball Association rules included a "pitcher's box."

early while the pitcher had the ball inside the box. The controversial call ended the inning and the Ramblers' rally.

Ford argued vociferously against the call until he was red in the face, to no avail. The Ramblers regrouped and blanked Detroit in the top of the seventh inning. Had the run counted in the bottom of the sixth, the Ramblers would've won the game in regulation.

Instead, the game went to extra innings. In the top of the eighth, the normally sure-handed Ramblers' second baseman, Al Berry, committed two rare errors. On one of those errors, pitcher Louise Miller took a throw while covering home plate and very nearly was knocked unconscious by the incoming Detroit runner.

"I remember that after we lost that game, 3–1, we rode to the hotel on that old bus. We cried all the way back to the hotel. We should've won that game."

In the end, the Ramblers finished the tournament in third place. In a wire to the hometown *Arizona Republic* newspaper, Ford wrote: "We still have a bad taste in our mouths. We don't feel that a pitcher is in position to pitch with no one to pitch to."

All these years later, Dot still had that fiery look in her eyes. "That's the moment when I truly began to hate umpires. They had too much say in the game. They changed the entire outcome of the game. The game should be decided on the field, not by some wrongheaded call like that."

• • • • • • •

After stopping along the way back to Phoenix to play several exhibition games to raise gas money for the trip home, Dot returned to high school from those first world championships in mid-to-late September. Her classmates were weeks ahead of her in school.

"That didn't bother me a bit. I never was much of a student. I just wanted to hang out with my friends."

One of those friends was a boy named Tommy McBrayer. Tommy, a good-looking, freckle-faced classmate, was the brother of one of Dot's young acquaintances. Whereas Dot never invited her female friends over to the farm, she had no such compunction when it came to Tommy.

"All my friends had working bathrooms in their houses. Where was I going to tell the girls to go, the outhouse? I was embarrassed about the lack of indoor plumbing. With boys . . ." Dot left the rest unsaid.

"I taught him how to catch birds in a trap and stuff like that. We'd go out in the fields at the farm and set a trap. The doves would go into the traps to get the food, and then we'd shoot them. We'd build a wood fire and have a pan and just cook and eat them. We used to do that, because when you were my age at home, you didn't have that much to do.

"But that's how I met Tommy. And he was serious. You know, he really liked me." Dot sounded surprised by this.

"He and I used to go roller-skating quite often. He'd call me, like on Friday night and say, 'Let's go.' And we'd go. I guess he thought he was my boyfriend. I didn't feel that way about him, but he was fun to spend time with. I suppose I went with him because that's what all my friends were doing. It was expected."

All this was innocent enough, and Dot thought nothing of it until Tommy asked her to go the school's formal ROTC Military Ball with him. "I guess I must've said OK, but I never even knew what it was. I had no clothes to wear to a thing like that. I was wearing jeans. He came to pick me up; he had a bouquet of flowers and I said, 'Tommy . . .'

"I had to tell him I didn't have any clothes to go to something like that. And he said, 'OK. Come on, let's go skating.' We went to an indoor rink out in Mesa or somewhere. Everybody used to go. There were a lot of people there, music, I'm sure. So, I guess that's where we went on that day we were supposed to go to the Military Ball. Tommy was all dressed up in his uniform. I felt terrible. I don't know why my sister didn't alert me or somebody didn't tell me what it was all about. But I had no idea. That was probably a big thing. Most of the girls went."

All these years later, Dot still sounded miserable about ruining Tommy's date. "I was just a poor farm girl. What did I know about such things? All I cared about was playing ball."

• • • • • • •

In the off-season, Dot continued to occupy her non-class hours with tennis, volleyball, basketball, roller-skating, swimming, diving, and, on increasingly rare occasions, riding Babe. The year before, Ford had told Dot that she was overextending herself. He gave her a choice: continue to pursue diving and swimming or play softball.

For Dot, there was no decision to be made. When March and April rolled around, she happily laced up her metal cleats and once again took the field for the Ramblers. The team practiced under the lights at University Park and played their games on weekend nights.

For away games, the team traveled by automobile, most often in a three-car caravan. "We drove all the time and Ford . . . I don't know how he did it, but there was no GPS at that time and we'd get lost once in a while. We'd just follow him wherever he went. He drove ahead and he usually took all the rookies with him or some of the older players. We had to sit up there and talk to him to keep him awake. We drove a lot at night because time was of the essence.

Dot packing the car for a softball road trip, circa 1940s. *Courtesy of the Dot Wilkinson Collection*

"Being on the road was not the easiest thing. We drove in cars that didn't have any air conditioning in them, back and forth between Phoenix and California and Phoenix and Fresno and up in Oregon and all over the place. We stayed in fleabag motels or wherever we could find. Way back then, there weren't very many motels, so we had a hard time finding a place to stay. So we did a lot of driving at night.

"You just did nothing. You went into a motel, and you went out to eat at a certain time in the afternoon, you played ball, and you went home, and that's it. It wasn't all the glorified good times that people think you had. So many nights, we drove all night to get home so we could go to work or school the next day.

"It wasn't easy, but I wouldn't trade any of it. It was fun. Now I think back on it, and it was fun. Back then, it wasn't too much fun. Softball was fun, but it wasn't easy way back when.

"Ford used to think when we were out on the road so many days that we should get out and stretch our legs. Even if we had to play catch in a field, we would. I can remember practicing in an old field more than once. You'd just get out and play catch, loosen up, because driving in the car wasn't the best thing in the world."

• • • • • • •

For the second consecutive year, the Ramblers won the state softball championship. That feat gave the team the right to represent Arizona at the 1938 World Softball Championships, but the final state series cost the Ramblers the services of their regular catcher, Norma Acuff, who suffered a season-ending injury in a home plate collision.

Without a replacement to fall back on, Ford called in Dot right before the world championships and handed her a catcher's mitt—or a "round doughnut," as Dot called it. "I got back there the first time and I caught. I didn't have anything but a glove, and they let you do that. I didn't have a mask or a chest protector."

Ford gave Dot some on-the-spot guidance. "He said, 'You're the catcher; you run the team. You're in a position to see everything that goes on. You can call every play; you can do the whole bit. That's the place to be.'"

Dot caught her first game in 1938 when the Ramblers' regular catcher got hurt in a game. For the next twenty-seven years, Dot ruled behind home plate. *Courtesy of the Dot Wilkinson Collection*

He modeled Dot after the Chicago Cubs catcher at the time, Gabby Hartnett. "Ford said, 'That's the way I'm teaching you.' And he did. He used to just tell me little things. . . . 'Do this, or sit there, or do that, or do whatever.'

"And, when I first started, I had a little fat glove, a round doughnut. That was tough to catch pop flies with when you had that glove. I tried to push it off on the first baseman or the third baseman but they didn't play as close to the batter as they do nowadays, and it was too far for them to go to make the catch."

The moment she squatted behind home plate for the first time, at just sixteen years old, Dot became the field manager for the Ramblers, their permanent catcher, and, in short order, the greatest catcher ever to play women's softball.

Dot was in charge of calling the pitches via hand signals (the majority of pitchers threw only a couple pitches: a rise ball and a drop ball, or changeup). She dictated the location of the pitches by positioning her glove where she wanted the pitcher to target the pitch. She also aligned the fielders for each batter and controlled the flow of the game.

The other significant change for the Ramblers before the World Softball Championships was the addition of a player from a competing local team. Ford added to the Ramblers' championship roster the dark-haired, sturdy, big-hitting pitcher/outfielder Amelina Peralta.

With these key changes in place, Ford and the team left for Chicago via automobile before dawn on September 1. According to a daily log of the trip kept by pitcher/outfielder Margaret Vance, on the first night, Ford checked them in at an auto court in Albuquerque, New Mexico. The second overnight stop was Oklahoma City. After a workout the morning of September 3, the Ramblers drove to Tulsa, where they stopped long enough to chalk up a 6–4 win in a night exhibition game against a tough Tulsa team.

The caravan arrived in Chicago late on the morning of September 6. According to Vance, that night, Ford arranged for his players to go to the movies. "We went to the show to see *My Lucky Star* with Sonja Henie. It cost us 90 cents. It was a good show but not worth 90 cents."

Over the next two rainy days, the Ramblers worked out in the mud at Grant Park. For Dot, this was a period of great adjustment. For the first time, tournament officials were requiring the catcher to wear a mask and a chest protector.

"On our first trip back to the world tournament after I started catching, I had to learn how to wear equipment. I had to wear a protector because it was a law; it was a rule. . . . But I didn't want to wear it. Ford picked up the equipment at our stop in Oklahoma City.

"That chest protector is in the Hall of Fame because it's a laugh. I just got a small one, and I cut it all the way around and took the padding out of it so that it was just like a piece of cloth. But it was legal. They said I had to wear it, so I did.

"Everybody would say, 'Don't you ever get hit in the middle or under the protector and get hurt?' I'd say, 'No, that's what I have a glove for. You're supposed to catch the ball.' I never got hit in the chest, for crying out loud. . . . If it goes into your chest, you catch it. If it goes up high, you let it hit the umpire. That's why I was a sitting-down catcher. Just squat as low as you can and sit down there. If it goes over my head, let it hit somebody else."

On September 9, the skies finally cleared enough for the Ramblers to play their first game. They faced a daunting opponent. The team from St. Joseph, Missouri, had compiled a regular-season record of 57–1.

At the end of the regulation seven innings, Louise Miller and the opposing pitcher were still knotted in a scoreless tie. The Ramblers had strung together seven hits over those seven innings, including two by Dot in her three trips to the plate. But it wasn't until the ninth inning, when outfielders Lois Pitts and Velma Grubbs belted a pair of home runs, that the Ramblers clinched the victory.

The next night, the team squared off against Oklahoma City. The Ramblers drew first blood with a run in the fourth inning and added three more in the fifth and sixth innings. Unfortunately, the lead didn't hold up. Their opponents roared back with a run in the sixth and three more in the bottom of the seventh to tie up the game. As a result, Phoenix was pushed for the second consecutive game into extra innings. They scored a pair of runs in the top of the eighth. Once again, Oklahoma City rallied at the last possible moment to knot the game at six, which sent the game into a ninth inning. This time, after Lois Pitts cracked yet another home run, Oklahoma failed to mount a comeback. The Ramblers scored a 9–6 victory, moving them into the quarterfinals, where they would have to play the Nebraska state champions, a team that had compiled an impressive 33–3 record in their regular season.

The rain earlier in the tournament had wreaked havoc with the game schedule. The Phoenix-Nebraska game got underway at seven o'clock on the evening of September 10.

After the Ramblers easily dispatched Nebraska by an 8–0 score, they were forced to wait around for another four and a half hours to play the semifinals against J. J. Krieg of Alameda, California.

By this time, close to midnight, Dot already had caught twenty-five innings in a little more than twenty-four hours, and her friend and pitcher, Louise Miller, had pitched the same number of innings. Still, the pair held off Alameda for five innings. The Ramblers clung to a 2–0 lead going into the sixth inning, when Alameda plated a pair of runs to tie the game.

Phoenix failed to score in the top of the seventh. That left an opening in the bottom of the last inning for the California team. They pushed across the winning run on an error at first base and a triple. For the second straight year, the Ramblers' hopes were dashed by one run in the semifinals.

According to Dot, this time on the way home, Ford expressed his disappointment not with the umpires but with his team. "You let yourselves get beat by a bunch of girls in tennis shoes," he spat, referring to the white cleats worn by the Ramblers' opponent.

Dot was more determined than ever to bring home a championship next time. But, in the meantime, the team was off on their barnstorming tour, beginning with the two-game, record-setting exhibitions against the New York Roverettes in Madison Square Garden, New York City.

On these trips, the games were heavily promoted, tickets were sold, and the visiting team generally was guaranteed a negotiated, fixed fee for their appearance.

Following their back-to-back extra-inning victories and to generate more funds to cover their expenses for the road trip home, the Ramblers stopped in Cleveland, Ohio, for a pair of games against two former world champions, the 1936 champion National Screw and Manufacturing Co. team, and the 1935 champions, the Weaver-Wall girls.

· · · · · · ·

In the fall of 1938, Dot arrived late back to Phoenix Union High School for her senior year. By her own admission, she wasn't applying herself in school beyond doing the minimum to graduate. Outside of school, she was coming into her own both on and off the field; no longer a scrawny colt, Dot was becoming an attractive young woman.

Her friend, the Ramblers' longtime shortstop Jean Klont, was dating a young man named Al Dalmolin. By the 1938 season, Al and his friend, Raymond G. "Spud" Harris, had become fixtures at Phoenix Municipal Park, one of the local fields at which the Ramblers practiced and played games.

Before long, Spud asked Dot out, and the two became an item, often double-dating with Jean and Al. "I guess I thought going out with Spud was the thing to do. I don't know. So I went out with him. We never went anywhere real special that I can remember. He used to come to the house all the time. He'd come for Sunday dinner. He'd play cards with my folks and stuff.

Dot and Raymond G. "Spud" Harris, circa 1938. *Courtesy of the Dot Wilkinson Collection*

"When he'd come out to the house, he'd want me to have his car the next day. So I'd drive him out to his job—he worked nights at the state hospital [Phoenix Mental Hospital] at 501 North Twenty-Fourth Street—drop him off, and take the car to school the next day."

And so Dot fell into a routine. She'd pal around with her girlfriends and spend time with Spud on the weekends. She remained the top seed for the high school tennis team and played volleyball and basketball to fill in the months in between.

But Dot was anxious to make some money. A few years earlier, in 1935, as part of the New Deal, President Franklin D. Roosevelt had heeded the advice of his wife, First Lady Eleanor Roosevelt, and signed an executive order creating the National Youth Administration (NYA). Mrs. Roosevelt had been particularly concerned with the plight of unemployed youth. With the NYA, the impetus was to employ young people between the ages of sixteen and twenty-five—in other words, young women just like Dot. So when an opportunity to work under the NYA presented itself, Dot jumped at it.

"I got assigned to the Garfield Services School. It's still over there, at Twelfth Street and Roosevelt. We got maybe ten or fifteen dollars a month for going there and working with the kids."

As fate would have it, another young woman, Kathleen "Peanuts" Eldridge, and her friend Margaret Thrift, also applied for NYA positions at the same time.

"I was going to Phoenix, and they were going to St. Mary's. We lined up wherever the folks doing the hiring told us to, and we just ended up in the same place. That's how we met."

Peanuts was fun and funny, and Dot was instantly drawn to her. The feeling, as it turned out, was more than mutual. "I was pretty stupid. I was a farm girl, and that was it. That's why I got caught with Tommy not having any proper clothes to go with him to the ball and that kind of thing. Nobody ever talked to me—my mother never talked to me about any of that stuff. Why my sister didn't, I don't know. But I don't know whether my sister ever went to the functions at high school or not. . . . Probably not, because we didn't have any money. We didn't have the clothes, so we didn't get invited to those things."

Dot pursed her lips and narrowed her eyes as she reached back through the decades to capture an elusive memory.

"This is way back in the back of my mind. Somebody I went to high school with had me stay with her one time, and she was trying to show me . . . teach me how to kiss. I remember that. I was pretty young; I guess it might have been early in high school. I can't remember who that was or what it was, but I remember I wasn't impressed. I had no idea that that meant anything. She was just trying to show me how.

"I didn't think about that even, until I did. Peanuts kissed me and then from then on. . . . But I didn't think about being gay or straight or whatever. I mean, I knew what it was. I knew I liked it, and I liked her.

"It was just like . . . maybe Spud would kiss me or I'd kiss him or whatever, and that didn't move me at all. But Peanuts one time did, and that was different. I could tell the difference. I mean you realize that there's something different. I knew right away. And so it kind of stayed that way."

Dot and Peanuts circa 1939. *Courtesy of the Dot Wilkinson Collection*

Peanuts, who lived at home with her folks and her brothers and sisters, became a regular fixture at Dot's house. She would stay overnight every Friday night she could. If Dot's folks thought anything of it, they never said a word.

Spud, on the other hand, was less pleased with Dot's dwindling time and attention. The time Dot spent with Peanuts, Margaret, and Dot's other friends took away from the time he and Dot had together. Still, he wasn't ready to give up, nor did Dot discourage him entirely, either.

Spud continued to vie for Dot's heart, even as it became clear he was fighting a losing battle.

· · · · · · ·

For the sixth consecutive year, the Ramblers rolled over the local competition, and for the third consecutive year, that earned them the right to represent Arizona in Chicago at the 1939 World Softball Championships.

The Ramblers and several of the team's players were undergoing transformations. Dot's good friend, star pitcher Louise Miller, got married early in the season and became Louise Curtis. The Ramblers picked up another superstar player from the local competition, the versatile outfielder Margie Wood (later Law). As for Dot, she finished up high school at the end of the 1939 school year, and Ford convinced her to enroll in Phoenix Junior College for the fall.

As they had done in previous years, the Ramblers barnstormed their way across the country en route to the tournament to fund their travels. They stopped first in New Orleans for a three-game set with the powerful Jax Brewers and promptly got thrashed three times.

Next, the girls moved on to Memphis for a series with the Tennessee state champions. Here, they had better luck. Louise had recovered enough from a sore arm to limit the opposition to five hits. Margie Wood stole home when the Memphis catcher got lazy on a throw back to the pitcher. Amy Peralta and Dot slammed consecutive doubles. The game went into extra innings, but in the end, the Ramblers got back in the win column with a 4–2 victory. It was the first time Memphis had lost a ball game all year.

The next night, against the same Memphis team, Dot was on fire. She banged out three hits, including a game-winning blast that shattered the record for the longest round-tripper ever hit by a woman at Hedges Field.

After one last 9–1 routing of a team from Carbondale, Illinois, it was on to the Ramblers' third world tournament appearance in the Windy City.

An easy win over Birmingham behind the strong pitching of Peralta on Saturday morning, September 9, set up an evening battle of the titans with Dot and company staring across the field once again at the Jax Brewers—the same Jax team that had crushed the Ramblers three straight times less than a week earlier.

Naturally, the Jax were heavily favored to win this time too. Luckily, the Ramblers never paid much attention to prognostications. Louise Curtis, well used to pitching under pressure, did not disappoint. The Ramblers scratched out a run in the second inning on three hits, and Louise held them steady the rest of the way. The 1–0 shutout gem propelled Phoenix into a semifinal matchup with Louisville, a team that had upset the previous year's runner-up, the Chicago Down Drafts.

After barnstorming their way to Chicago, struggling with their hitting almost the entire way, and playing back-to-back games the day before, the Ramblers seemingly had nothing left to give. Louisville jumped out to a 2–0 lead in the first inning. Phoenix, facing the fastest hurler they'd seen the entire season, failed to get on the scoreboard until the seventh inning. Peralta beat out an infield hit. Velma Grubbs followed with a double that moved Amy to third base. Jean Klont brought Amy home with a sacrifice fly. Unfortunately, Louise grounded out, stranding Velma on second base with what would have been the tying run.

For the third time in three trips to the world championships, the Ramblers left Chicago empty-handed. Dot was miserable. "I hated losing. We all did. It just felt horrible. And then you've got to wait a whole year to get back there and try again."

Dot riding in style past the PBSW store as part of the 1940 victory parade after the Ramblers captured the World Softball Championships for the first time. *Courtesy of the Dot Wilkinson Collection*

Part Four

HITTING HER STRIDE

12

Coming into Her Own

By the time Dot and the Ramblers returned to Phoenix from the 1939 tournament, Adolf Hitler and the Germans had invaded Poland, and World War II was underway. Change was in the air for Dot as well, as, thanks to Ford's generosity, she began her freshman year at Phoenix Junior College.

The transition to higher education didn't make Dot a better student. If anything, she became even more lackadaisical about her studies. Her closest friends, including Eleanor Firpo, joined her at the junior college, and together they regularly cut classes to seek out fun.

That year, a traveling troupe of entertainers showed up in town, set up a tent on Van Buren Street, and performed a "Walk-a-Thon."

"They were all-night things, people that danced all night and performed. It was a show. They traveled all around the country. They'd stay for a month or so in one area and they'd get people all involved like we did when we were going to college.

"We used to cut school to go out there to watch them perform. We'd all start out at the college and by the time noontime came, we would say, 'Let's go to the Walk-a-Thon.' So, we'd take off.

"What they'd do is, there were probably maybe ten or so couples and sometimes they'd walk together, sometimes they'd walk separately, and they'd have marriages as part of it . . . They'd have all kinds of different stuff. They'd all perform and sing and dance. It was really just a traveling show.

"We used to go to that Walk-a-Thon a lot, and we got involved with two of the performers. After it was all over, we took them out to South Mountain and rode horses with them.

"That was just an interesting time. Just that one year, that was it. I never went to another one afterwards because they never came back again, I guess. But it was just a matter of entertainment . . . something to do. They had thousands of people that came every day and night. It was open twenty-four hours, because you could go there any time to check on them and make sure they were up walking. This was a big contest with them. It was just a really fun time."

Attending the Walk-a-Thon with Firpo, as Dot always called Eleanor, also led to Dot taking up another sport—a sport that eventually would make her almost as famous as softball. "That's where I first started bowling, because Firpo said one day when we got back from going out to the Walk-a-Thon or . . . she said, 'Let's go bowling.' And I said, 'I don't know how to bowl.'

"And so that's when she showed me how to bowl. We went bowling down at the Gold Spot on Central Avenue, across from the Westward Ho hotel. . . . When I was in college, when I first started, it would have been once a week, probably on a Thursday night or something like that. You just went down there and picked a ball up out of the thing. Finally, you got your own. Sixteen is the heaviest, and when I finished, I had a fifteen and that was my mistake. I should have gone down, because it got to where my fingers couldn't hold it. But I liked it, so I kept it."

And so, the school year progressed with picnics at South Mountain, bowling nights, and the Walk-a-Thon as long as it was in town.

· · · · · · ·

When April 1940 arrived, Dot put down her bowling ball and broke out her cleats again. Ford forbade his players from bowling during the season, and Dot wasn't one to go against anything Ford said.

By this time, the Ramblers' reputation as a softball powerhouse was firmly established. Girls and young women from all over the greater Phoenix area came to try out for the team. One of those girls, fourteen-year-old Jessie Glasscock, proved to be a great find at shortstop and quickly became Dot's close friend.

The Ramblers got off to a torrid start at the beginning of the 1940 season. Dot was seeing the ball better than she ever had, hitting at a pace well over .300, and commanding the team from behind home plate. From the first pitch in March/April through the end of the regular season, the team was virtually untouchable.

That year, for the first time, the state tournament would be double elimination format, so that a team that lost once would get bounced into the losers' bracket. If that team lost a second time, it would be out of the tournament. The other rules change extended the state championship finals from a best-of-three to a best-of-five series.

Twenty-five teams vied for the Arizona state title. In the end, the Ramblers proved victorious, earning them the right to represent Arizona in the 1940 World Softball Championships, to be held in Detroit, Michigan. It was the first time the tournament would be played outside of Chicago.

13

The 1940 World Softball Championships

WHEN DOT AND COMPANY set off by car on their barnstorming trip to Detroit for the 1940 World Softball Championships, war was raging in Europe. Poland, Denmark, Norway, the Netherlands, and Belgium had fallen. Benito Mussolini recently had joined forces with Hitler. France had surrendered next, and the Blitz had begun with the bombing of England.

At home, Dot's family kept up with the news of the day on the radio and in the local newspaper, but not Dot. She was singularly focused. After three consecutive losses in the semifinals from 1937 to 1939, Dot and her teammates were more determined than ever to bring home the title.

At the outset of the barnstorming trip, the Ramblers took two straight from the Omaha team but suffered a key loss when Margie Wood sprained her ankle in the second game. She was expected to be unable to walk for at least six days and would miss the rest of the run-up to the tournament. On top of that, since the players roomed together in larger groups while on the road, most of the team had come down with colds.

After the second game in Nebraska, Ford and the team pushed on, driving all night to arrive in Chicago in time for a game the following night against the Chicago Hydrox team.

As luck would have it, that game was postponed by one day due to rain. When the Ramblers and Hydrox did take the field, they battled into extra innings—four of them. In the end, the Ramblers strung together four runs in the eleventh inning to take the game. They followed that win with another the next night and arrived in the Motor City with a few days to spare.

Miraculously, when the Ramblers took the field on September 7, 1940, for the first game of the tournament, Margie was back in the lineup.

"Ford was a genius at taping injuries. We could sprain an ankle one game, and he'd tape it up for the next so we could play on it."

In the end, the Ramblers played two games that day. The *Arizona Republic*, the local newspaper, covered the action:

> *If the PBSW Ramblers of Phoenix had breezed into town on pinto ponies and brandishing six-shooters, they couldn't have been much more effective as the women's division of the national softball tournament swung into action here today.*
>
> *The Ramblers, who swept up from the sun country like a prairie fire, defeating all the opposition they could unearth on the way, went into the thick of the tourney fight by eliminating the South Bend, Indiana entry, 8 to 2. The Ramblers defeated Lansing, Michigan, 2 to 0 Friday.*

Louise pitched that first victory, then gave way to Amy, whose windmill delivery led to consecutive shutouts in the quarterfinal and semifinal games (2–0 versus Oklahoma and 4–0 against St. Paul, Minnesota). With that victory in the semifinals over the St. Paul team, the Ramblers broke their three-year semifinal jinx and propelled themselves into the finals for the first time in their history.

Threatening skies hovered over University of Detroit Stadium on Monday, September 9, 1940, as Dot and her teammates prepared to take the field against the formidable Koch Furnitures of Cleveland. But those dark clouds were nothing compared to the storm brewing in Dot's heart.

Ford announced that he planned to send Amy to the mound against Cleveland. Dot sought out her manager. "Louise is our number one pitcher. She should be the one to throw."

"Dot, do you want to win this game?"

"Of course I do. What kind of question is that to ask?"

"Well, if you want to win this championship, then Amelina needs to pitch."

Dot opened her mouth to object again. Louise was her friend. Louise had been the Ramblers' mainstay on the mound since the beginning of the team.

Ford cut off Dot's protest. "Don't argue with me about this. Louise is exactly the same kind of pitcher as the Cleveland girl. That team has six players with previous tournament experience. They're used to hitting the type of balls Louise throws. We need Amy's slingshot delivery. Cleveland's never seen anything like that. And that's how we're going to win."

Dot stomped off, but when it came time to take the field that night, she put on her game face and crouched behind home plate to receive Amy's first pitch. Louise played the tenth fielder position.

The Ramblers jumped out to a quick 3–1 lead after the first two innings. Then, in the top of the third inning, with first baseman Esther Holton on third base, Louise on second, center fielder Midge Holly at the plate, Dot on deck to bat cleanup, and no outs, the heavens opened up, and heavy rain soaked the stadium and everyone in it. The umpires called the game and decreed, per tournament rules, that it would resume the next night exactly as it stood.

Dot and the rest of the team returned to their hotel, where they cleaned up and got warm. The 3–1 lead was nice but certainly not insurmountable.

Tuesday, when the teams took the field once more, the rain had passed, but the temperature was a chilly fifty degrees. Louise and Esther resumed their spots on second and third, respectively. Midge and Dot accounted for the first two outs of the Ramblers' third, but Amy rapped out a single. Cleveland committed one of their eight errors in the game, and just like that, Phoenix cleared the bases, upping their run total to five.

In the fourth, Mildred Dixon and Louise worked out walks sandwiched around a Jessie Glasscock single, and Esther added another single. That accounted for three more Rambler runs.

The following inning, Dot and Margie Wood drove in the last two Phoenix tallies.

Amy was in top form on the mound too. Her fastball flew by the Cleveland players; she held them to just six hits for the entire game. In addition to her RBI in the fifth, Dot went one-for-three at the plate and scored two of the Phoenix runs.

When the dust settled, the Ramblers won, 10–3. It was the most lopsided championship game in the history of the tournament. Dot, who received one of her nineteen career All-American designations following the game, apologized to Ford for doubting his game strategy. Amy, who also was named All-American, received a standing ovation from the crowd of five thousand when she stepped forward to collect the individual radio trophy each of the Ramblers received as a memento of their triumph.

At long last, the PBSW Ramblers were softball royalty and the state of Arizona had its very first national champion in any sport. On Monday, September 16, the whole of Phoenix turned out to celebrate the victorious team.

The festivities began at 11:30 AM, with an automobile parade through the city. It stretched from Central Avenue and McDowell Road, past the Ramblers' loyal sponsor, Peterson, Brooke, Steiner, and Wist's store, and on to city hall. Dot rode atop a convertible, waving to the crowd along the way. Her smile lit up the town.

At high noon, the team and Ford were welcomed on the steps of city hall by the governor of Arizona, the mayor of Phoenix, and a host of other dignitaries.

The next night, the Phoenix Chamber of Commerce put on a huge banquet at the Westward Ho in honor of the team. As Dot and her teammates entered the banquet hall, everyone rose to their feet and cheered.

The governor handed each member of the team an individual trophy—a small, working radio with a gold figure of a softball player on each end. Then, in another surprise, the players and Ford were each presented with a brand-new luggage set.

"I was eighteen years old, and that was the greatest time of my life. It still is. Nothing before or since has ever topped winning that tournament."

14

The War Years

THE RAMBLERS' CHAMPIONSHIP WIN in 1940 set the Arizona softball world on fire. Young women and girls came from all over town to vie for a spot on the team. Peanuts tried out for, and made, the lineup. "Ford liked her, and so she played for us. She was a pretty good hitter. She never could run fast, but she played right field and then she ended up staying with the Ramblers afterward and kept score. She always was there."

Jessie Glasscock brought one of her neighbors to audition for Ford. She was a young schoolteacher named Virginia "Dobbie" Dobson. With the retirement of Esther Holton following the 1940 season, the Ramblers needed a first baseman. Dobbie, who was tall and lean with remarkably long legs, was perfect for the position, and she was a very capable outfielder as well.

Other 1941 additions to the team included infielder Shirley Judd (later Wade) and Charlotte "Skipper" Armstrong (who later played for the Queens and for the South Bend Blue Sox in the All-American Girls Professional Baseball League), whose trick behind-the-back pitch regularly fooled opponents.

1941 PBSW Ramblers team photo. Top row, from left to right: Pauline Crawley, Lois Green, Wanda Law, Mickey Sullivan, Virginia "Dobbie" Dobson (later Bickle), Margie Wood (later Law), Jessie Glasscock, Shirley Judd (later Wade). Bottom row, from left to right: Zada Boles, Jean Hutsell, Louise (Miller) Curtis, Amelina Peralta, Mildred (Woods) Dixon, Dot Wilkinson, and Kathleen "Peanuts" Eldridge. *Courtesy of the Dot Wilkinson Collection*

Ford wanted to be certain to have his team in place and ready to compete just in case he couldn't be there to see the 1941 season through. He had arrived home from the Ramblers' championship victory in Detroit to the news that, like all American men between the ages of twenty-one and forty-five, he would have to register for the draft. Ford was thirty-two at the time.

Once the initial rush of excitement and attention at being the champions wore off, Dot fell back into a routine. She, Peanuts, Margaret, Jessie, and now Dobbie, would bowl in weekly leagues.

"We all moved from the Gold Spot to a bowling alley downtown called the Pla-Mor. They had a bar there, and of course everybody liked that better than they did the Gold Spot. Of course, we always started in the bar that was in the front and then moved to the bowling lanes. Bowling was a fun thing. So, you know, it was just something to do at night.

"We enjoyed it. We had a lot of fun bowling because we still had all of our friends and we still went out and did whatever we wanted to do, and bowling was just some reason for us to get together. We started out just bowling one night a week, and then we ended up bowling two nights a week, and you know . . . during that time, we won a lot of stuff. We all got to be pretty good. We won the league a few times and we won things. I won singles."

In addition to the bowling, the friends found other ways to amuse themselves. "We'd go to drive-in movies once in a while and we took in most of the movies. We used to do that together, all five or six of us. We'd all try to get enough money. . . . Like, on one night a week they had a cheap night that you could get in for eleven cents. We would say, 'We've got to have sixteen cents apiece by Tuesday night.' That was enough for an ice cream cone for five cents and a ticket to get into the movie.

"Sometimes, some of us couldn't come up with it. So, we'd go out and sell Coke bottles, or anything, to get to go. None of us had any money, but that's what we did to take in all the movies.

"We used to go to the Orpheum Theater a lot. We used to sit up in the balcony and put our feet on the railings. It was good. And sometimes, when we were young, I think even a few times we siphoned a little gas out of somebody else's tank. We didn't sell it. We put it in our car so we could have it in the one we were running around in. We didn't have money to buy gas. But we never took all everybody had. We just took a little.

"We took what we needed, because we used to go out to South Mountain and hang out, listen to the radio and dance or picnic there or at Blue Point, where we'd overnight sometimes, and we damn sure didn't want to be stuck out there. So, we'd get a little bit of gas and then go on about our way.

"Later on, we used to go all the time and pick oranges off people's trees or just randomly stop and find an orange grove. We did that when we had our horses. We would be riding, and we'd just go into a grove and fill up our sweatshirts full of oranges off the trees. Sometimes, we'd find where they were picking. They'd have a box filled with oranges. We'd take the whole box and pay for them.

"And sometimes, we'd stop in the watermelon fields and help ourselves to a watermelon and then go to the canal. We'd get in the canal and swim and have cut up watermelon.

"One time we did that, and the guy that owned the watermelon field came, and here we were skinny-dipping in the canal. He stood over our clothes and wouldn't let us get out for a long time. So we didn't go back to that field again.

"We girls didn't have anything to do. So we did little things like that. We didn't hurt anybody. We had a lot of fun when we were young. But we manufactured all our fun, because we didn't have any money."

· · · · · · ·

Meanwhile, also on the home front, things were getting more complicated for Dot. Spud, who had been waiting all these years for Dot to make a full commitment to him, was growing impatient. The more time Dot spent with Peanuts and their group of girlfriends, the more jealous and disaffected Spud became.

Finally, he confronted Dot. "I started going with the girls more and more—all of us. Well then, I think Spud wised up. He was a little older than I was. He said, 'Well, if you . . . if that's the way it is with you, then it's time for me to get out.' So, he enlisted [on January 7, 1941] and shipped out. He spent four years in the army [Spud was discharged on June 23, 1945], and he wrote to me all the time. But he knew I was gay when he left. That's why he left.

"We didn't talk about it. He just knew when I told him I was going with the girls more, he knew it. And he just . . . I don't know, it was just something he knew. If he'd been mad about it or upset about it, he wouldn't have left me his car when he went to the war. But he did, and we remained friends. We were always friends.

"I didn't start going out with him again or anything when he came back, but we were just always friends. He just came to the house and visited all the time, whoever I was with. He still came to see me. He was a nice guy, and I was happy for him when he got married. And when he died, his wife called me.

"She told me, 'Well, my husband thought an awful lot of you.' And I said, 'Well, we've been good friends.' And she said, 'I was glad he had you for a friend.'

"And that was it. My parents never questioned why Spud didn't come around anymore. They just accepted whoever came to the house to spend time with me."

In addition to Spud's dramatic exit, Ford was pushing hard for Dot to go back for her sophomore year at Phoenix Junior College. She wasn't having any of it. Dot wanted to make money.

In February 1941, Margie Wood heard that Goodyear was building a plant on the west side of town and ramping up production of airplane parts for the military. The company was taking applications. Margie; Dot; Peanuts; several other fellow Ramblers; Dot's friend, Flossie Ballard of the Queens; and Peanuts' friend, Margaret Thrift, got hired. They were among the one-third of America's women who were working by the end of the war.

Dot's job was to run the drill press. Her preferred style of dress (jeans) fit in with factory attire during the war. She was making real money for the very first time, she was having fun with her tight-knit group of friends, and she was free to be who she was.

Still, Ford tried to convince her to go back to school. "He said, 'Dot. You have to get an education.' He was always promoting schooling for all of us girls. He even paid for some of our college tuitions. He offered to pay for mine again. I said, 'Ford, I'm making more money than I've ever made in my life. I don't want to go back. I'm going to keep working.' He finally gave up on me and left me alone about it. He knew I wasn't going to do it. But he wasn't happy about it."

• • • • • • •

The 1941 softball season rolled around with the reigning world champion Ramblers heavily favored to repeat. They were the darlings of the news media, especially in their home state.

But while their exploits on the field made headlines, Dot, Peanuts, Jessie, and Dobbie managed to keep their private lives to themselves. "We were born at a time when we were all in the closet, and that was just the name of the game. You had to live with it, and that's what we did."

Dot said this matter-of-factly, with neither animosity nor bitterness. Homosexuality was illegal in Arizona, as it was elsewhere in the country, but that was of little consideration to Dot. She loved whom she loved and went about living her life without self-recrimination or regret.

The team ripped through the competition all summer long. Raymond F. Law of the Associated Press wrote an article about the Ramblers that was printed in newspapers across the country under the headline: NATIONAL GIRLS SOFTBALL CHAMPS STRESS YOUTH, VERSATILITY, FIGHT. Dot was the main focus:

> One summer evening in 1934, during a girls' softball game out in Hollywood, an 11-year-old kid came to bat for the Ramblers from Phoenix.
>
> Serving 'em up for Hollywood was Lois Terry, the "blonde bomber," then considered the greatest pitcher in the game.
>
> Quite unimpressed, Dot Wilkinson, the fifth grader from the desert country, socked the ball out of the lot for a home run which (a) won the game; (b) got her an offer to go into the movies, which she didn't accept, and (c) put the Ramblers in the big time softball picture which they now dominate as national champions.
>
> That was the second year of the club's existence. The 1941 Ramblers, who will defend their title in the national tournament at Detroit September 10–14, also emphasize youth, plus unusual versatility of players and a tradition of winning that seldom is broken. The average age of the 10 regulars is 19 years.
>
> They are real champions. They take all comers. This season has seen a parade of the west's toughest teams to Phoenix, all to take a drubbing from the Ramblers, who, between invasions, have taken time for a few triumphant tours of their own ...

And, later on in the article:

[The Ramblers] have never lost more than eight games in any one season. For eight years, the record stands 317 won, 38 lost. . . .

"It is not a team of stars," Hoffman insists, although the roster includes Dot Wilkinson, now 18* and without a peer behind the plate. . . .

They are great "money" players. The first five hitters, Louise Curtis, Mickey Sullivan, Dot Wilkinson, Amelina Peralta, and Marjorie Wood, take pleasure in murdering the tightest pitching any team can throw at them.

Squad members are carefully selected, for many qualities, chief of which, in Hoffman's estimation, is the feminine equivalent of intestinal fortitude.

When I related the portion of the article about her home run off of Lois Terry, Dot's recollection was crystal clear, and she laughed. "I would hardly say I belted the ball. Lois Terry was the best pitcher in the world. She was so fast I couldn't even see the ball. I hit left-handed, so I stuck my bat out there and made contact—and the speed of the pitch against my bat propelled the ball over the third baseman's head. They weren't expecting me to hit it that way, so it went a long way. I could run pretty fast, so I just kept right on running until I crossed home plate."

As always when she told me a story from almost ninety years ago, I kidded with her. "I can't remember what I had for breakfast yesterday, but you can recall a specific hit from 1934."

"I can't remember what I had for breakfast yesterday either, but hitting a home run off Lois Terry isn't the kind of thing you forget."

"And the movie offer?" I asked. "Surely that's the kind of thing you'd remember too?"

Dot shook her head. "I probably never even knew about it. I'm sure Ford said no on my behalf. He was very protective of all of us players."

Without further ado and with a shrug, we went back to talking about the aftermath of that first championship run and the 1941 season.

---

* In August 1941, when this newspaper article appeared, Dot was 19 years old.

The *Arizona Republic*, the Phoenix-based newspaper, printed a massive team practice photo of the Ramblers in its Sunday Sports section. The caption partially read: "Winner up to yesterday of all but one of their 35 games this year, the PBSW Ramblers of Phoenix, greatest feminine softball team Arizona has ever produced, are heading down the home stretch toward defense of their world championship six weeks hence in Detroit."

That single loss was to the Ramblers' archrivals, the Queens. Subsequently, the Ramblers took the other two games of that three-game series.

Later on, the caption says: "Crouched behind the bat is Dot Wilkinson, undoubtedly the nation's outstanding feminine softball catcher and a top-notch slugger with a current .446 average."

If Dot was fazed at the time by the enhanced scrutiny, the publicity, and the expectations, she didn't show it. As always, she was singularly focused on one thing: winning. And so it came as a massive blow when the Ramblers were shocked in the first round of the 1941 World Softball Championships by the up-and-coming New Orleans Jax.

In front of a crowd of eighteen thousand fans in University of Detroit Stadium, the Jax pushed across the lone run of the game in the first inning against Amy Peralta. Jax shortstop Olympia Savona scored on an infield single by Lottie Jackson. The Ramblers mounted a challenge in the bottom of the last inning, when they had both the tying and winning runs on base. But Dobbie flied out to end the game and the Ramblers' hopes of repeating as champions.

• • • • • • •

Even as events on the field hadn't turned out the way Dot had hoped, on the personal front, the 1941 softball season was life-changing for her. It wasn't so much that Dot fell out of love with Peanuts; it was more like her friendship with Dobbie simply evolved into something far more significant.

"When somebody asked me when I kind of made a change-over between Peanuts and Dobbie, I don't know how that happened or when it happened. I know Peanuts used to come and spend Friday nights at my house once in a while before, and then . . . Dobbie came on the team in '41 and I don't know how that [falling in love with Dobbie] happened.

Dot continued, as if trying to puzzle through it herself. "I had Spud's car, and I was most often the one driving when we all went out anywhere. Dobbie's parents' house was closest to mine, so she always was the last one in the car with me. Eventually, we just sort of became a thing.

"We were still all friends; we still all went out together to the bars and dancing and doing our things, and we were all just friends. I don't know how Dobbie and I got started."

But "get started" they did. Dot and Dobbie remained an item for fifteen years. "Dobbie got her own car after so long and so she just started

Dobbie and Dot
(foreground) and
friends, at South
Mountain, circa 1942.
*Courtesy of the Dot
Wilkinson Collection*

Sometime in 1941, Dot ended her relationship with Peanuts and took up with Dobbie. Still, Peanuts and Dot remained lifelong friends, and the three women often spent time together. *Courtesy of the Dot Wilkinson Collection*

dropping by. She'd come by the house. She stayed a lot of times. If her parents were drinking, she wouldn't stay home. And I never stayed much at her house, either, because they just had a two-bedroom house. And all they had between their bedroom and Dobbie's bedroom was the bathroom. So there was no way that I wanted to stay there, and she didn't want me to stay there."

Despite her romantic relationship with Dobbie, Dot's friendship with Peanuts never wavered.

"Well, shucks, Peanuts and I remained friends until the day she died. In 1998–99, she developed cancer and had an open wound on her abdomen. I dressed that wound every day, and it was not easy. But I talked to her, and I got to tell her, I said, 'Peanuts, you know I've always loved you, and you're the best friend I ever had.' And she was; we remained friends forever."

· · · · · · ·

When the Japanese bombed Pearl Harbor on Sunday morning, December 7, 1941, Dot and her parents listened to the account on the radio. As the United States entered the war, her work and that of the others at the Goodyear plant took on more of a sense of urgency.

Still, not much else about Dot's life changed. She remained fully focused on softball. Opening day for the 1942 season had been scheduled for April 20 at the Phoenix Softball Park.

For the first time since they began competing, the Ramblers weren't the prohibitive favorites to win the Arizona State Championship. As a result of their 1940 win, they'd been exempt from playing the state tournament in 1941. Instead, they received an automatic bid to the world event. That opened the door for their archrival, the Queens, to step through.

Going into the 1942 season, the Queens held the state crown, and they showed no inclination to give it back to their crosstown rivals.

Around the country, softball boomed. Families, fans old and young, working-class and affluent, filled ballparks, hungry to watch the women play. Games between the Ramblers and the Queens sold out, and the enmity between the two teams, including among their respective fans, reached nearly fever pitch.

"When we played at the Phoenix Softball Park against the Queens, that was dog-eat-dog with the teams and the same way with the fans. Our fans would be on one side, and their fans would be on the other. When I'd come up to bat, they'd boo me. When they came up to bat, our fans would boo them. That's just the way it was."

Dot said this nonchalantly, but there was no question that she took the heckling personally. "This one guy in the stands behind home plate razzed me all through a game. I told him, I said, 'If you don't quit razzing me . . . when this game is over, you'd better get out of here, because I'm coming after you.'

"Well, he just kept on and kept on, and after the game was over, I started out after him. He ran into the men's room, and I went right in after him. I kept right on going. At that time—that was when I was very young—I had my little fat glove, and I popped him across the head, and I walked out of the men's room."

The sportswriters loved Dot and her fire for the game.

Miss Wilkinson is rated one of the best feminine softball catchers in the nation.

When the chips were down and the country's top feminine teams were battling in a recent national tourney, a runner attempted to steal second base on Phoenix. The bullet peg from the comely Miss Wilkinson cut her down—the fifth time the catcher had turned the trick that day.

Umpires officiating in that tournament agreed the girl was the greatest feminine catcher they ever had seen in action.

The article goes on:

Said to have one of the greatest competitive spirits in girls' softball, she hits best when runners are on the bases, and is deemed one of the most dangerous batters of the nation's feminine stars. Her lifetime batting average is well above the .300 mark.

Softball is not the only sport in which she has starred. She was the girls' tennis champion at Phoenix Union High School, and won the state title. She formerly was a diving star on the University Aquatic Club swimming team.

The article was accompanied by a staged action shot of Dot flipping off her catcher's mask to make a play on a foul pop. The caption underneath the photo read: "All-American catcher is agile Dot Wilkinson, star of the Phoenix Ramblers, shown here going after a high foul. The Arizona girls will seek their second National title later this month and Dot is expected to aid them greatly in their efforts."

· · · · · · ·

Predictably, both the Ramblers and Queens reached the finals of the state championship tournament in late August. For the first time, rather

More often than not, Ramblers manager Ford Hoffman (or Dot in his stead), would hire a photographer to take staged "action" pictures, which Dot would then run over to the local newspaper in order to get publicity for an upcoming game. *Courtesy of the Herb and Dorothy McLaughlin Collection, Greater Arizona Collection, Arizona State University Library*

than a single game to decide the winner, the finals were to be a best-of-five series.

For the first game of the state championships, the Ramblers sent Amy Peralta to the mound against the Queens' ace, Carolyn Morris (who later pitched for the Rockford Peaches of the All-American Girls Professional Baseball League from 1944–46). Morris had trouble with her control that first game, and the Ramblers walked over the Queens, 9–2.

The next night, Ford tapped Skipper Armstrong to pitch. She held the Queens to two hits, and the Ramblers won, 5–2. They were one win away from the state championship.

In the third game, Dot had a hand in both Ramblers' runs, smacking an RBI double and scoring the other run, but the Queens staved off defeat. The score was Queens 3, Ramblers 2.

Still, the Ramblers had the upper hand going into Game 4 of the series, and they took full advantage of it. With three runs in the first inning, two in the fourth, and another in the fifth for good measure, the Ramblers once again claimed their place as the best women's softball team in Arizona.

Because of the war and subsequent travel restrictions and gasoline shortages, the Amateur Softball Association (ASA), the governing body for softball, determined that rather than each state sending a champion to the world tournament, it would divide the country into fifteen regions. Each state winner would vie for the regional title and the right to go to the world championships, to be held again in Detroit in mid-September.

As a result of the drastic reduction in teams competing for the title, the ASA also changed the format of play to double elimination. Any team losing one game in the tournament would be moved to the losers' bracket. A second defeat would send that team home for good.

The Pacific Coast regional tournament to determine which team would advance to the World Softball Championships in Detroit was far less suspenseful. The Ramblers made short work of the Utah Copperettes in three straight games and prepared to avenge their world tournament first-round loss from the previous year.

After the win, as they often did, Dot, Dobbie, and Peanuts headed out to celebrate. "We never went to gay bars, although a few of them existed.

We just went to regular bars—the 902 (902 East Van Buren), and the 307 (307 East Roosevelt). At the 902 we would play pool and shuffleboard. The 307 was a little nicer place, a little dressier.

"We used to go to Patrick's Park too, a straight bar down here in South Phoenix at Thirty-Fifth Avenue and Broadway. They let us dance together and just do our own thing. They just thought we were a bunch of friends having fun, and most of the time that was the way it was.

"We used to go there after the ball games. They had a big room out in the back, and they'd let us dance. Dobbie was a good dancer. She's the one who taught me how to dance. Peanuts loved to dance too, and so we all danced together."

And then the girls would get back to playing softball.

In Detroit, the Ramblers went about their business with their usual intensity, battling through to the semifinals, where they would face the New Orleans Jax and red-hot pitching sensation Nina Korgan, the same pitcher who'd humiliated the Ramblers and sent them packing in the first game of

Peanuts takes her turn at indoor shuffleboard at the 902 while Dobbie (foreground) looks on. *Courtesy of the Dot Wilkinson Collection*

the championships the previous year. Since that victory, Korgan had been mowing down all the other tournament competition too. In fact, she had thrown six consecutive shutouts dating back to last year's championships.

This year's semifinal game, originally scheduled for Saturday, September 19, 1942, was postponed due to weather. On Sunday, Ford tapped Skipper to take on the undefeated Jax. Although she held the Jax to just two hits, Korgan blanked the Ramblers except for Dot's single with two outs in the seventh inning. As that was their second loss in the tournament, once again, the Ramblers returned to Phoenix empty-handed.

Dot felt wretched. That misery was replaced by shock when she returned from the tournament to discover that her mother, tired of the lack of indoor plumbing and the hardships of living off the land, had sold the family farm. "I came home from the ball trip to discover that she'd sold the place for $3,800 and closed a deal for a house with indoor plumbing and a bathroom. I have no idea whether or not that was a good price for the farm, but Mother obviously thought it was since it made the purchase of the new house possible."

The new house was located at 103 North Twenty-First Avenue. "It was at Twenty-First Avenue and Adams, right on the streetcar track. The streetcar ran on Adams Street to right there. So, people would get off the streetcar and end up on my porch if they'd been drinking too much and they didn't know where they were. My father would sit down with them and drink a beer."

Dot didn't care about the vagrants; the house had indoor plumbing.

While her parents were getting them settled in the new place, Dot returned to work at the Goodyear plant. But she and some of the other women were dissatisfied with the working conditions. In November, Dot and Peanuts decided to organize a walkout over equal pay.

"We got high on our rooster or whatever and decided that the women were taking the bad part of the deal. Goodyear was hiring guys in there for more money than we were making, and we were having to teach them. So, we were going to go to bat against them.

"All the girls—there were about eighteen of them there that all worked in that department . . . drill press and all of those kinds of men's jobs.

I worked on a big press thing and different things. And we all decided, 'We're going to tell them they're either going to have to pay us more or make the guys learn from somebody else.'

"When we got down to the nitty-gritty, well, the only ones who quit were me, Margaret Thrift, and Peanuts. The three of us walked out. The rest of them stayed working there."

Now cast out of Goodyear, the three women needed jobs.

"That was when Jessie Glasscock's father was a field man for lettuce, and we thought we'd just go to work for him. So we did.

"First day after we got out of Goodyear, we worked in the field. Well, we found out we didn't like that too good. It's hard work. It was hard on your back, and you had to get down on your hands and knees and pick the lettuce.

"So, we told Jessie's dad, 'That's not going to work for us; it's too hard.' I don't think Peanuts and Margaret even went back for the second day. I did. But the third day, I went back into the shed and cut the tops off the lettuce.

"Well hell, the next day after that, I couldn't even . . . my hand wouldn't move. It was so sore from using that knife all day. So, I thought, 'That's not what I want.'

"But we had fun learning that skill."

Still, the trio needed paychecks. Arizona, and Phoenix in particular, were becoming home to a variety of military-related manufacturing operations. Defense contractor Garrett AiResearch had just finished building a brand-new plant on the back side of Sky Harbor Airport.

AiResearch, originally based in the Los Angeles area, would use the Phoenix facility to manufacture its revolutionary cabin pressurization system for the B-29 bomber as well as oil coolers for the B-17 and the B-25.

In an interview with the local paper, Thomas Darlington, the manager of the new facility, said, "The particular type of employees the company will need to begin with are skilled machine-tool operators, precision inspectors and assemblers, tool makers, designers and production control men.

"It is expected many of these jobs can be filled by women."

Timing favored Dot and her friends. Had the war not created extraordinary opportunities for women to step into traditionally male jobs, it's hard to say what Dot might have done for money. As it was, Dot, Margaret Thrift, and Peanuts were in luck. "All three of us went over to AiResearch, and we got hired on there.

"I was lucky. I had an easy job at AiResearch; Peanuts had a tough one. She had to lift these big old things and drill them. . . . Meanwhile, I'd sit up on the counter and throw pipes through a machine or something. She used to come by and say, 'Oh, nice that you get the easy job.' So, anyway, we worked together out there, but that's it."

Dot and Peanuts continued working at the AiResearch defense plant for the remainder of the war, but the terms of employment were challenging.

"When we would tell them, 'We're not going to be here tomorrow or the next day,' because we had a ball trip—a game Friday night, a doubleheader Saturday, a game on Sunday and an all-night drive to get back home to Phoenix—well, we got fired. They wouldn't give us a couple of days or anything. We'd just lose our time.

"But then on Monday morning, when we'd come back, we'd just walk in the door and go back to work. You were just rehired all over again, just the same as it was at Goodyear. You'd lose your seniority every time, but who cares about that? Nobody would give you the time off to go play ball. That's the way it was. It wasn't easy, but we did it. I would've done it anyway. I wouldn't have cared if I ever got a job back. I wanted to go play ball. So, I did."

• • • • • • •

The truth, however, was a little more complicated. While Dot only wanted to play ball, she didn't want to play for just any team. At the close of 1942, a group pulled together by the Chicago Cubs owner, Philip Wrigley, came up with a plan to fill the hole left by so many male baseball players going off to fight in the war.

Wrigley and his associates recognized the growing popularity of women's softball and dreamed up a brand-new, hybrid model of ball to be played in a new league they would form in the Midwest. At first, Wrigley called the league the All-American Girls Professional Softball League. Before the season was halfway over, he would rename it the more familiar All-American Girls Professional Baseball League, made famous in the 1992 Penny Marshall instant classic film, *A League of Their Own.*

Over the course of several years, the size of the ball decreased from the regulation softball (twelve inches in circumference in 1943) to the size of a men's major league baseball (nine-and-a-quarter inches in the early 1950s). Also, by 1950 the pitchers in this new league were required to pitch overhand from fifty feet instead of underhand from forty feet.

Wrigley's first order of business was to recruit the best female ballplayers he could find to fill out the league's initial four teams. Spring training was set to get underway on May 17, 1943, so there was no time to waste.

Predictably, Wrigley's search brought his representatives to Phoenix. "They came out here to Arizona and offered some of us contracts. We went up to the Westward Ho and they put out some contracts to different players. They wanted to give me $85 a week [the maximum at that time] to come back there and catch. Well, I had no interest in that at all. For one thing, I didn't want to leave the Ramblers. I'm a homebody; I wouldn't want to leave home anyway. So I never did.

"I played against a lot of those gals you saw in the background of that movie . . . Carolyn Morris [who pitched for the Queens], Pauline Crawley, and Skipper Armstrong [both of whom spent several years with the Ramblers and the Queens] all went from Phoenix. The rest of us didn't go. There were several on our team that went up to that meeting at the Westward Ho. But we just didn't go. We didn't want to go. We weren't interested."

In addition to staying loyal to the Ramblers, Dot strongly objected to the rules of Wrigley's league and the fact that the organizers were most interested in sweeping under the rug any hints of lesbianism among the players. The gals were required always to wear their makeup and lipstick. The uniforms were more feminine skirts. Off the field, each girl/woman was assigned a chaperone (this applied even to young women in their twenties). There was to be no "fraternizing" with players from other teams. And, perhaps most galling of all to Dot, the players were required to attend charm school to learn how to behave, to properly apply makeup, and how to act more feminine.

"Those girls who went to Wrigley's circus had to check in like they were in college or something. I just wasn't interested, period. Some of those girls who went back there to Chicago got themselves in trouble by breaking curfew and fraternizing with other girls. Lots of them snuck around in order to be who they were. Some of them got caught and dismissed. None of that was for me."

The expression on Dot's face as she related all this made clear her disgust.

"On the Ramblers, we didn't have a dress code of any kind when we weren't on the field. We didn't pack a dress when we traveled to play ball. We wore Levis and whatever we had."

On the subject of the movie, Dot became even more animated. "Everybody thought that gal catching in the movie was me because her name was Dottie. Well, I've had to answer that question so many times, that sometimes I'd say, 'OK,' just to stop the conversation. It was not me, and I didn't have anything to do with it. The movie was interesting, but I didn't want to have anything to do with it."

Dot shook her head and returned to the topic at hand—the ongoing seesaw battle with the Queens at home and the Jax on the national scene. The Ramblers had added a couple of new players—Zada Boles in 1942 and Pauline Crawley at the start of the 1943 season. The team prided itself on filling out its roster with all local talent.

Meanwhile, the Jax and Queens recruited the best players they could lure away from other teams. For the Jax, that was the Savona sisters, Freda and Olympia, and Nina Korgan, the pitcher they'd enticed away from Tulsa after she'd won them the national title in 1941. For the Queens, well . . . their manager, Larry Walker, wanted anyone who could look pretty in the uniform and wasn't afraid to stick it to the rival Ramblers.

That number included some of Dot's longtime friends. "Flossie Ballard played first base for the A-1 Queens, and their coach, Larry Walker, told his players, 'Don't ever slide into Wilkinson at home plate, because she blocks the plate. Just knock her down when you come in.'

"In this one game, about six people had already knocked me down. So, here came Flossie, and she knocked me down. So I got up and knocked her down. The umpire, old Art Van Haren Sr., just said, 'OK, ladies. That's enough.' Flossie went one way and I went the other, and that was it. He didn't kick either one of us out.

"She was my best friend. We always bowled together and everything."

Flossie was on the record about her run-ins with Dot as well. "Dot wasn't a poor sport, but she wasn't good at losing. I spent the first half of my life trying to beat her in softball and the last half trying to beat her in bowling."

Later in the same 1999 *Arizona Republic* interview, Flossie recalled what she termed Dot's "obsession" that the Queens were sliding in spikes-high on her at the orders of their manager. The Queens' first baseman said she paid the price another time while scoring on an inside-the-park home run.

"She [Dot] blocks the plate [which was perfectly legal]. I try to go around her, she trips me, the ball is nowhere around, she whim-whams the heck out of me. Everybody booed her for 10 minutes. That's the only time I ever saw her get booed.

"You'd better slide or take her out because if she had the ball, she had that base. She played with all the intensity you should play a sport with."

Without knowing what Flossie said in that newspaper article, Dot more or less confirmed her friend's recollections. "Ford would say to me, 'I don't care how good a friend Flossie is or Firpo is—you put the ball on them. Don't mess around.' So I learned from that that you have to play the game. Nobody is your friend when you're playing.

"Flossie and I would joke about it afterwards. She always told me her husband, Sam, liked me better than he liked her. Sam used to root for me when Flossie and I played against each other. He'd root for me every time I came up to bat. I'd say, 'Sam, you're getting in trouble.'

"When he had Alzheimer's and he would come to watch me bowl, Flossie would rib me by saying, 'He's cared more about you than me his whole life.'"

Queens catcher Lois Williams also had her share of run-ins at the plate with Dot:

> *I remember one Queens-Rambler game in 1943 when Dot had just sent our Nonie Thomas flying when she tried to score. I was boiling mad about that, and I made up my mind to run over her when I came in from third.*
>
> *I came roaring in a minute later, but Dot just dropped her shoulder at the last second and I went head over heels. I was out, too. . . .*
>
> *She got me plenty of times, though. . . . Once she barreled into home with her head down and broke my hand.*
>
> *But do you know who was the first one to the hospital to see how I was? Dot Wilkinson!*

· · · · · · ·

Beyond the distraction of the new All-American Girls Professional Baseball League forming to the east and the rough-and-tumble on the field, Dot was forced to take on new responsibilities. Ford, who always had taken care of and arranged everything for the team, had been drafted into the navy. He'd departed for training in San Diego on December 11, 1942.

Although he managed to get leave in time for the state tournament finals against the Queens and the world championships in Detroit at the end of the summer of 1943, it fell to Dot and a couple of the veterans to manage the Ramblers during Ford's absence throughout the season.

"We had a wonderful coach . . . Ford just took care of everything. I never thought about anything until I had to handle things myself."

"Handling" things included dealing with contentious fans anytime the Ramblers and Queens squared off. "This one game, this lady kept bugging us, and she was sitting right behind our dugout. There was a water fountain right there next to the dugout. She kept bugging us and bugging us, and finally, she said, 'You shouldn't even be playing out there. You come from the wrong side of town [south Phoenix].' I put my thumb on that faucet. She was sitting in the box seats, and I just soaked her. She let me alone after that.

"A game or two before that, a lady that worked next door to me got in a fight up there in the stands with another woman who was a Queens fan, and they were hitting each other with their purses, and everything was happening." Dot waved her arms around as if mimicking a wild fight. "So they [the fans] got serious."

Things became even more tense when the Ramblers and Queens battled in the best-of-seven state championship series in 1943. The Ramblers took game one on the strength of Amy Peralta's no-hit shutout.

Ford Hoffman instructing the Ramblers at an impromptu practice while on the road to the 1943 World Softball Championships. *Courtesy of the Dot Wilkinson Collection*

Ramblers ready for a road trip, 1943, Dobbie and Dot, top right.
Courtesy of the Dot Wilkinson Collection

The Queens fired back with a 6–0 victory in game two, and another masterpiece 1–0 win in game three. When the Queens also took game four, giving them a 3–1 advantage in the series and pushing the Ramblers to the brink of elimination, Ford, who was on leave from the navy, pulled Dot, Dobbie, and the rest of the Ramblers aside.

He called a meeting under the bleachers at Phoenix Softball Park. "His face was ashen. He said, 'Listen. I pulled some strings and already bought train tickets for the trip to Detroit. I got you all listed as recruits to get you on the train. I can't get my money back. We have got to win this championship. That's all there is to it.'

"Well, we all felt horrible. None of us wanted Ford to lose his money, so . . ."

So, the Ramblers took the next two games to even the series at three games apiece. The sixth game came down to extra innings. Peanuts led off the ninth inning with a single. Pauline Crawley, who came in to pinch-run for Peanuts, scampered home on Dot's game-winning double.

Finally, in the decisive game seven, the Ramblers pulled out an extra-inning win once again. Ford heaved a sigh of relief, and the team boarded the train to Detroit the next day.

Unlike in previous years, in 1943, the Ramblers went directly to the tournament. There were no barnstorming stops along the way to pay for the trip and to tune up. The team arrived, checked in to the hotel, practiced, and got down to business.

All the while they were winning, they kept an eye on the Jax and Nina Korgan, who was busy mowing down the opposition. Predictably, the Ramblers ran headlong into the Jax not once but twice. The first meeting lasted eleven innings, with Korgan limiting the Ramblers to four hits. Only two Ramblers runners reached second base, both with no outs, but they could advance no farther. They lost the game, 1–0.

With the double-elimination format, the team got a reprieve by beating Detroit. That earned them the right to face the Jax the next day. If the Ramblers could win this game, they could force the Jax into one final matchup. If not, the Jax would be champions again.

In the end, the Jax ended the suspense early, piling up six runs in the third inning while their pitcher struck out nine and allowed only one hit.

Dot was not pleased.

· · · · · · ·

She was even less pleased in 1944, when the Ramblers easily won the state tournament from the Queens but had to scramble to come up with enough cash to make the trip to Cleveland, home to the world championships that year.

Despite the addition of rookies Jean Hutsell and Wanda Law, a first-round loss to Toronto meant that the Ramblers had to fight all the way back to reach the finals. And fight they did, through eight games in six days. Most satisfying was eliminating the Jax, 1–0, and winning a rematch against the Toronto team that had put them into the losers' bracket at the outset.

Unfortunately, the Ramblers ran up against a well-rested Portland, Oregon, team in the finals. The game, played just hours after the Ramblers won their semifinal tilt, lasted eleven innings, and the Ramblers succumbed to exhaustion and the victorious Portland team, 1–0.

• • • • • • •

Dot's very Democratic household mourned with the rest of the country on April 12, 1945, when President Franklin Delano Roosevelt passed away. The family celebrated together when V-E Day and the end of war in Europe arrived.

Dot's situation at work became less stable. Some of the men, freshly back from the fighting abroad, were reclaiming the jobs taken by the women during their absence. Ford hadn't yet returned from the navy, although fortunately, he'd never been sent overseas on deployment, either.

Ford and his wife, Peggy, owned a restaurant on East Van Buren Street called Hoffman's. Peggy was running the place. Dot temporarily took a job making the ice cream at the restaurant's separate ice cream counter when her job at AiResearch went to a returning GI.

The team continued to hold practices in preparation for the upcoming season. The Ramblers' lineup was changing. Mickey Sullivan, the team's original third baseman, left to join the US Marine Corps Women's Reserve. She was replaced by Shirley Judd (later Wade). Mildred Dixon and Louise Curtis left the team for a newly formed Phoenix squad called the Holsum Maids. Margie Wood, who had married the year before, continued to play, although she was now Margie Law. Dot felt the earth shifting beneath her feet on the field, where some of her closest friends were moving on.

Still, when the dust from the 1945 regular season settled at the end of August, it was the Ramblers and the Queens duking it out for the state championship. The regular-season series between the two archrivals had ended in a ten-games-to-ten tie.

For eight consecutive years (excluding 1941, when the Ramblers were given an automatic entry into the world tournament as sitting champions and thus didn't play in the state championships) the Ramblers had triumphed over the Queens. Could they do it again?

The atmosphere at the Phoenix Softball Park was electric. The players were tense. The crowd was on edge. In a subsequent feature article in the *Arizona Republic*'s *Arizona Magazine*, Clipper Williams described the action:

> *It was the 14th inning of a scoreless battle between the Denton Queens and the PBSW Ramblers for the Arizona girls softball championship.*
>
> *The hit-and-run play was on.*
>
> *Nonie Land, Queen second baseman, was taking a good lead off third base, having arrived there on a hit, an error and a passed ball.*
>
> *At the crack of the bat, Miss Land raced for home plate. The infield grounder was fired back to Dot Wilkinson, Rambler catcher, who put the ball on Miss Land, and the umpire called her safe.*
>
> *That started the fireworks.*
>
> *A score or more fans in the jammed Phoenix Softball Park cascaded onto the diamond, charging that Miss Wilkinson "elbowed" Miss Land when they collided at the plate. One middle-aged woman spectator was all for pulling out Miss Wilkinson's hair.*
>
> *Order was restored when members of both teams cleared the playing field of irate fans.*

In the end, the Queens handled the Ramblers with relative ease, winning the state title series 4–1.

For the first time since 1937, the Ramblers would not qualify for the World Softball Championships.

Just days later, the Japanese surrendered, thus ending World War II. Ford Hoffman, discharged from the navy, arrived home on October 5, 1945, four days before Dot's twenty-fourth birthday.

The Ramblers playing their archrivals, the Queens, in 1949. *Courtesy of the Herb and Dorothy McLaughlin Collection, Greater Arizona Collection, Arizona State University Library*

Part Five

AT THE TOP OF HER GAME

Keeping Her Eye on the Ball

POSTWAR PHOENIX WAS CHANGING, and so was Dot. The war years had prompted a boom in manufacturing jobs, and the population in the city was growing. So was the need for housing.

Ford, looking to take advantage of the times, got his real estate license and hung out a shingle. At the tail end of 1945, he opened Hoffman Realty, first in a small space at 823 East Van Buren, across the street from his restaurant. Not long after, he moved the office to 936 East Van Buren, a larger space directly next door to the family restaurant. Dot was one of his first hires.

"Ford did everything for me. He was like a father to me. I really wouldn't have what I have today if it hadn't been for him."

In truth, Ford's beneficence was both lifesaving and life-changing for Dot. In the postwar years, the vast majority of those women who had fulfilled heretofore "male" roles in the workplace were being forced via societal norms back into traditional roles, such as housework and child-rearing. Those women who did work outside the home were mostly

relegated to secretarial positions or teaching. Dot had neither the training, the desire, nor the aptitude to take on such jobs.

Ford understood this and no doubt realized that without his help and
intervention, Dot would struggle to make her way in the world. By bringing Dot into his real estate business, Ford effectively shielded her from
the expectations, pressures, and realities that confronted most young,
unmarried women of her age.

"I started by filing for him and doing office work. He taught me everything about real estate. He said, 'You're going to be the office manager.' He
put me in a position to learn. Pretty soon, I was head of the escrow department. I wrote the papers. I wrote all the contracts when we sold a house.
I had a notary license. We had a lot of payments there and I handled a
lot of money at different times. I went to the bank every day and did the
banking.

In 1945, when Ford Hoffman returned from war, he opened Hoffman
Realty. Dot was his first hire and his only salaried employee.
*Courtesy of the Herb and Dorothy McLaughlin Collection, Greater Arizona Collection,
Arizona State University Library*

"We had a couple of guys that would buy these houses and then we'd collect the mortgages for them. I remember a guy named Demere, he had a bunch of houses, and I remember writing checks to him. The customers would come in and pay at our office, and then I'd write checks to him.

"Ford taught me how to write the papers. We had five or six salesmen working out of the office, and I used to have to write commission checks and all of that. Then, in the late '40s, I got a real estate license. I was the only paid employee in the office. The rest of them were all salesmen. They worked on commission. I had a salary of something like $150 a month.

"Ford's business slogan was, 'The poor man's friend.' That was the slogan because he made it possible for poor people to buy houses. They could never buy a house otherwise, but Ford made it cheap so they could, or he made it so they could afford the payments."

• • • • • • •

In addition to taking Dot under his wing in business, Ford was determined to educate Dot on the business side of softball. In February 1946, Ford convened a gathering of several other team managers in Fresno, California. He took Dot and Dobbie with him to participate in the talks. After a nine-hour overnight session, Ford and his counterparts had hammered out the parameters of a brand-new regional softball league to cover the states of Arizona, California, Oregon, and Utah. The original teams in the Western States Girls Major Softball League (later called the Pacific Coast League) included the Ramblers, the Salt Lake City Shamrocks, the Buena Park Lynx, the Queens, the Fresno Rockets, and the Lind and Pomeroy (Portland) Florists (later Erv Lind Florists).

Art Funk, who had built the original Phoenix Softball Park, had just put the finishing touches on the $100,000, brand-new Phoenix Softball Park. The state-of-the-art stadium, located on Seventeenth Avenue at Roosevelt Street, "was constructed with softball in mind. With seating arranged to give all spectators a clear view of the action on the field, the park is capable of handling crowds of 5,000 to 7,000.

"Special dressing rooms and dugouts were designed especially for the park with tunnels from dugouts to dressing rooms. Trained groundskeepers put the field in shape for championship play, and keep it in the best possible condition throughout the long Phoenix playing season."

The new park would be home to the Queens. Meanwhile, the Ramblers claimed Phoenix Municipal Stadium, a spring training home to Major League Baseball teams, as their home field.

The first season of the league went smoothly, right up until the playoffs. The Ramblers won the inaugural season of the Western States Girls Major League convincingly. The league had a rule in place that even if a team had won the league regular-season title, if it lost its own state championship, it would not be eligible to compete in the regional tournament.

Before the start of the Arizona State Softball Championships, Ford, in his capacity as state softball commissioner and regional tournament director, ruled that the requirement be waived for that season. He insisted that all appropriate parties had agreed to the stipulation.

The Ramblers and Queens squared off in mid-August in the state finals. For the second consecutive year, the Queens walked away with the Arizona title, four games to two. The victory ensured the Queens a trip to the World Softball Championships, to be held in Cleveland for the second consecutive year.

The Ramblers, stinging from their defeat, went on to compete in the Southern Pacific Regional Championships, where they met and trounced the Buena Park Lynx. Dot and her teammates had a hard time concentrating on the field, however. Queens manager Larry Walker had protested the Ramblers' eligibility to play in the regional tournament since they had lost to the Queens on the state level. In essence, Walker declared that he never had agreed to the stipulation that a team that lost its state tournament could still be eligible to compete in the regional tournament.

The protest went all the way to the national governing board of the Amateur Softball Association, and for days, Dot and company waited to see if they would be going to Cleveland.

Finally, one week before the world championships were set to get underway, the ASA released its ruling. A cable addressed to the sports editor of the *Arizona Republic* newspaper read: "Phoenix Ramblers declared ineligible by world's championship committee. Committee also rules Phoenix Queens play a three-game series with California Lynx girls Saturday and Sunday, September 7–8. Winner only girls team eligible for world's championship from Southern Pacific region."

There it was. Dot vacillated wildly from being mad at the world to being inconsolable. But that wasn't the end of the story for 1946. A second telegram followed, addressed from M. J. Pauley, executive secretary of the ASA, to Ford Hoffman, Arizona softball commissioner:

"Report Phoenix Queens have overtraveled the official 15 working-day period permitted. Report they left Phoenix July 11 and returned August 7. This is 19 travel days or four days over allowed time. If true, according to your records, disallow Queens trip to 1946 world championship and notify Buena Park Lynx girls to proceed here and compete as 1946 southwestern regional champs."

The newspaper interviewed Ford, trying to unearth who had made the "anonymous" complaint against the Queens. Ford pointed out that his office (the Arizona Softball Commissioner's office) could not protest a travel time violation.

Dot insisted that she has no direct knowledge of who lodged the complaint against Walker and the Queens in 1946, but the glint in her eye made clear that she believed Ford, in his role as manager of the Ramblers, had a hand in it. Sometimes a little revenge can take the sting out of a bitter disappointment.

Since they wouldn't be going to the tournament and had time on their hands, Dot, Dobbie, Jessie, Peanuts, and assorted others decided to take a short vacation.

"We'd never had a vacation before. All our 'vacations' took place on ball trips. We borrowed a tent somewhere and set off for a campground up near Pinetop, Arizona. Well, none of us knew what the hell we were doing. We'd never been camping. So it took us forever to set up the tent. We finally got it up and got in it, and it started to pour down rain on us.

The tent collapsed on top of us; we had to fight our way out of it. We were soaking wet and laughing ourselves silly.

"Finally, we gave up trying to put it back up and drove about thirty miles into Lakeside. We got ourselves a cabin down there and stayed for a day or two before coming back home."

After that disastrous 1946 postseason, the Ramblers never missed the world championships again. That aborted camping trip was the last vacation Dot took during her softball-playing career.

· · · · · · ·

The fallout from the debacle of 1946 was swift and far-reaching. Larry Walker of the Queens was so incensed that he pulled them out of the Amateur Softball Association altogether and created a rival organization, the National Softball Congress (NSC).

To entice other teams to join his new league, Walker offered them a percentage of the gate, along with travel allowances and expenses for the players. He also ruled that professional players like those in the All-American Girls Professional Baseball League and the National Girls Baseball League based in Chicago, could join an NSC team without penalty. To emphasize the point, Walker convinced pitcher Carolyn Morris and slugger Merle Keagle to forsake the All-American Girls Professional Baseball League and return to the Queens to join the rest of his stable of stars.

Former Ramblers pitching ace Louise Curtis organized a new Phoenix team to challenge the Queens in the NSC. She called them the Maids, and she brought over former Rambler teammates Mildred Dixon and Jean Dalmolin to join her, along with a bevy of ex-Queens players, to round out her roster.

The ASA retaliated by informing its participating teams, including the Ramblers, that they would lose their amateur standing and be disqualified if they so much as scheduled a game with a "professional" team (i.e., like those belonging to the NSC).

Of course, the ASA's stance meant that the crosstown rivalry between the Ramblers and the Queens, an entertaining show that brought thousands of fans through the turnstiles for every game, was on ice. Every entreaty the Ramblers made to the ASA fell on deaf ears.

"So, the Queens and Ramblers spent the 1947 season resentfully eyeing one another from a distance because the ASA and NSC weren't on speaking terms."

For Dot personally, the consequences of all this tumult were earth-shaking. Before the start of the 1947 season, Ford sent a letter to Ralph Peterson, president of Peterson-Brooke-Steiner-Wist, informing him that he would be stepping away from the Ramblers for the 1947 season:

> Please be informed that effective as of this date [January 15, 1947], personal affairs will prevent my assisting with the PBSW Ramblers during the 1947 season in any capacity. With illness both of my wife and infant daughter requiring a major portion of my time, and my business taking the remainder, I do not feel inclined toward affording time for outside activities.
>
> Dot Wilkinson, who has served as your team manager for the past several years during my absence for military service, is adequately qualified and should be able to continue the team very successfully. Veteran players on the team can readily handle coaching problems.

Even today, Dot scoffed at Ford's explanation and affirmed that his decision to step back had everything to do with the 1946 kerfuffle and nothing to do with "personal affairs." She proudly informed me that Ford and Peggy's baby, Dorothy Louise Hoffman, born on November 25, 1946, was a healthy baby girl Ford and Peggy named after Dot and Louise Curtis. Dot also was quick to point out that she still worked in the real estate office with Ford every day. If she needed a sounding board, he was readily available to her.

Regardless, the public reality was that at twenty-five, in her fifteenth season with the Ramblers and the only remaining stalwart from the original team, Dot was fully in charge.

In the beginning of March, she held workouts at a local school. Team mainstays Amy Peralta, Jessie Glasscock, Shirley (Judd) Wade, Dobbie, Peanuts, Zada Boles, and Margie (Wood) Law attended. Mickey Sullivan, fresh back from the service, returned, this time to play second base. Shortstop Jean Hutsell, utility infielder Betty Harris, newcomers Delores Low, Marilyn Downs, and rookie backup pitchers Lily Lopez and Proxie Irwin finished off the 1947 lineup.

Margie, who had taken the 1946 season off to have her first child, would be alternating regular pitching duties with Amy. She threw such a fast rise ball that Dot was forced to abandon catching with a standard catcher's mitt (the doughnut).

For the rest of her career, she would use what she called her "five-finger glove," or fielder's glove, to catch. "I used a finger glove with Margie, because she was a rise-ball pitcher. She kept throwing the ball over my head. It's kind of hard to catch it with that little doughnut."

Dot worked hard to put together a schedule that would generate fan interest. The Fresno Rockets, powered by infield sensation Kay Rich and with a solid team, was angling to challenge the Ramblers for the Western States Girls Major Softball League crown. The former World Champion Lind and Pomeroy Florists team from Portland, Oregon, was itching to make it all the way back to the top. Buena Park, Salt Lake City, and a team from Van Nuys rounded out the in-league opposition.

But Dot knew, without a doubt, that she needed to bring in a bigger headliner—she needed the kind of big-time rivalry that would satisfy the town's lust for softball excellence and fierce competition. She needed the reigning World Champion New Orleans Jax.

Freda Savona, the shrewd player-manager of the Jax, was happy to accommodate. The Ramblers and the Jax set up multiple series to take place throughout the year. And put on a show they did.

"One time," Dot recounted, "I got into it with the gal from the Jax, Freda Savona, down at Phoenix Municipal Stadium. She came charging up to me with a bat. I wasn't mad; I thought she was. I didn't have any idea that was put up by the Jax to gin up the crowd, because I know I was never involved in anything that was put up.

"If I got mad, I was mad for a reason. I did not know that she was putting on a show. I didn't find that out until a long time later. But I took the bait. I got mad when she came at me. I wouldn't take anything off of anybody. I didn't care if she was twice as big as I was. [Freda Savona was five foot ten; Dot was five foot three.] We didn't get into real fisticuffs, just a big argument."

The argument, in fact, was heard live on the radio. Municipal Stadium was a baseball stadium. The softball diamond was superimposed on the grounds so that "home plate, the catcher and umpire backed up right against the screen (with a radio announcer behind it)," the *Arizona Republic* reported.

> Jax shortstop Freda Savona once came up, heard the umpire call, 'Strike one,' and told him what she thought of the call.
>
> The radio announcer, within four feet of all this, cringed and tried to cover his mike. One word led to another with Dotty and the argument became unladylike and strident. The radio announcer ended in a crouching position under a shelf, both hands around the mike to shut out everything he could and talking rapidly to drown everything else out.

Increasingly, Dot got a reputation for being a hothead. She was not above kicking dirt on home plate while mouthing off to an umpire (whose job it was to keep the plate brushed clean). Her combative attitude and competitive fire only served to make the Ramblers more dangerous.

"One incident I remember in Fresno, California . . . instead of playing seven innings, we were playing nine up there in Fresno. So we had this big argument in the seventh inning. I thought the game was over, and I went out and I grabbed that umpire out at second. . . . I grabbed him by the shirt and shook him and said . . ." Here, Dot gestured animatedly, and her eyes gleamed with laughter as her voice trailed off, leaving her exact word choices to my imagination. "The game was still *on*. I thought the game was over. It was for me." Dot threw her head back and laughed with delight. "It's funny now. It wasn't so funny then."

When I pressed her to share more specifically what she yelled at the umpire, Dot equivocated. "I don't remember what I said. I remember grabbing him by the shirt collar and shaking him."

Dot didn't get fined or docked. "They kind of liked it because it brought more people to the ballpark. Another fifty-cent admission."

In late August, after securing the Western States Girls Major League regular season title, the Ramblers drew the tough Orange Lionettes and their second-year pitching sensation, Bertha Ragan (later Bertha Ragan Tickey) in the battle for the regional championship. Ragan had beaten the Ramblers all three times they'd played her.

In the end, the Ramblers bested Orange on consecutive nights to take the title and earn the right to represent the region in the World Softball Championships to be held again in Cleveland.

Upon arriving in Cleveland, the Ramblers had no trouble disposing of Iowa (1–0) and Texas (4–1). That set up a showdown with the Jax, who also were undefeated at that point in the tournament. Of the thirteen times during the regular season the Ramblers had played the Jax, Nina Korgan had shut them down nine times.

Once again, Nina and the Savona sisters prevailed, this time in a 1–0 shutout. Nina held the Ramblers to just one hit.

The loss knocked the Ramblers into the losers' bracket, putting them in the precarious position of having to win every game to stave off elimination. They took out their league rivals, the Fresno Rockets, in a lopsided 8–0 romp and followed that up with 3–0 drubbing of Toronto and a convincing 4–1 win over Columbus, Ohio.

After six games—fifty-one innings, the most played by any team in the tournament—Dot and company found themselves in the finals. Unsurprisingly, the team in the opposing dugout was the New Orleans Jax.

Nina Korgan was riding an eight-game shutout streak going into the game. The night was freezing cold—for a Phoenician. The temperature was forty-nine degrees, and the Ramblers' short shorts and uniform tops were not meant for those conditions. Behind the plate, Dot's fingers were stiff.

Three times the Ramblers had the lead, and three times they gave it away. In the end, Nina notched eight strikeouts against the Ramblers in the final, and although Phoenix nicked her for four runs, the Jax emerged victorious, 6–4. For the fifth time in their history and the third year in a row, the Jax were the champions. Dot accepted the runners-up trophy for the Ramblers, conceding that the Jax had played a better game . . . again.

The next day, the Jax announced their intention to play a ten-game World Series in Phoenix against the Queens, who had nabbed the rival National Softball Congress World Championship.

The executive committee of the ASA voted to rescind the world championship from the Jax, arguing that by scheduling games against an NSC team, the Jax had turned professional. The ASA vacated the Jax title and awarded it to the Ramblers, making them the 1947 champions by default.

The Jax responded by pulling out of the ASA and joining the NSC. They went on to hold their series with the Queens.

Dot was glum, as a picture of her with the 1947 championship trophy attests. "We didn't earn it. We didn't want the trophy that way. We didn't feel like champions. The Jax won fair and square, and they were amateurs at the time we played the game."

Dot appealed to the ASA. She requested permission for the Ramblers to play the Queens in a post-championship cancer fund–benefit series.

The ASA replied: "Ramblers are world champs and should rest on their laurels for the balance of the season. Arizona should appreciate the international recognition received. Don't by any means play NSC champs or title will be revoked and given to Toronto (the team that finished third behind the Ramblers in Cleveland)."

It would be years before the ASA would reverse itself and reinstate the Jax as 1947 world champions.

16

We Are the Champions

THE BAD BLOOD CONTINUED into the new year. The ASA knew it had to do something or risk losing more quality teams. Prior to the start of the 1948 season, the ASA ruled: "The game of softball is too universally played and too popular, so, therefore, professional players may play with or against amateur players without affecting the status of the amateurs. This is possible through authorized closed league competition which the ASA recognizes and provides for those who are not amateurs."

The softball powers that be in Phoenix selected Art Funk, owner and manager of the Phoenix Softball Park, to mediate a settlement and solution. He brought together Ford and Larry Walker and hammered out an agreement. A new "closed" league would be formed in Phoenix. The headline in the local newspaper, the *Arizona Republic*, explained: CITY SOFTBALL TRUCE IS TOLD.

The Girls Major League, unaffiliated with either the ASA or the NSC, would consist of the Ramblers, the Queens, and the Maids. All games would be played in the Phoenix Softball Park and a city champion would be crowned at the end of the season. None of this would have any impact on the Ramblers' regular Western States Girls Major League ASA-sanctioned play, the ASA World Softball Championships, nor on the NSC competition and its World Championship.

The Ramblers still would be prohibited from playing any "professional" team from outside that closed loop, including the Jax. But the rivalry between the Ramblers and the Queens would be alive and well and played in front of rabid fans of both teams in a state-of-the-art stadium.

Ford decided to officially return to the Ramblers to resume his management of the team's affairs off the field, but he left Dot in charge of everything that happened between the foul lines.

The Queens went on a shopping spree, recruiting every professional player they could get their hands on. They brought back Charlotte "Skipper" Armstrong, onetime Rambler and former Queens pitcher. Walker also lured in a couple from Chicago—Estelle "Ricki" Caito, lately of the Parichy's Bloomer Girls from the National Girls Baseball League, and Kay Rohrer, formerly of the Rockford Peaches and the Chicago Blue Bells.

Dot vaguely recalled that she had squared off against Kay when the latter played for the Bank of America team in Hollywood in the mid-1930s. They both were young teenagers at the time, and Kay was a rising starlet under three-year contract to Metro-Goldwyn-Mayer Studios.

When Kay broke her wrist playing first base in a softball game just as she'd begun filming her first picture, MGM gave her an ultimatum: she could be a movie star or a softball player but not both.

For two years, Kay abided by the studio's edict. She'd cost them a lot of money when she broke her wrist. But she was inconsolable. "I was 16 or 17, and I'd just lost my mother. I didn't understand people well then, but I felt at home on a softball diamond." Kay chose softball.

The Ramblers and Queens were set to clash in a three-game series to be played May 1–4, 1948. Newspaper columnists prognosticated over which was the better team. Fans snapped up game tickets to the Phoenix Softball Park.

The series did not disappoint. In the first game, the Queens' Skipper Armstrong pitched a one-hit shutout gem, and Kay Rohrer drove in the winning run in the bottom of the seventh inning. The Ramblers fired back in game two, scoring a 3–2 win. In the game three nailbiter, Dot slammed

Kay Rohrer, playing for the Bank of America team in Hollywood while under contract to MGM Studios in the mid-1930s.
Courtesy of the Dot Wilkinson Collection

a triple and scored the game's only run when Amy Peralta singled her home. The Ramblers collected another win the next night to take the first series, three games to one.

Ricki and Kay, especially Kay, took note of Dot. And Dot took note of them. They all struck up a friendship, even though such inter-squad camaraderie was strictly forbidden by the Queens manager.

"Kay and Ricki and Dobbie and I and Peanuts, and all of us. . . . They went out with us. They weren't supposed to because they played for the Queens, so we all used to hide when we were doing stuff together. Kay and

Ricki lived in an apartment. I lived at Twenty-First Avenue, and they were in an apartment on about Seventeenth or Eighteenth. I used to drive by there. Kay would be out in the front yard watering, and I'd stop and talk to her on my way to work. They went with us on a few picnics to South Mountain.

"We were up to South Mountain one time, and Kay made a point that she was after me. In that first year, when she was here with Ricki, she made a point that she . . . I don't know whether she just kind of had a crush on me or what it was. I don't know, but that's when we started talking. Of course, I never thought anything about anything."

But Ricki, Kay's girlfriend at the time, did, Dot related. "We all did stuff together, only Kay was the one that was the friendly one—Ricki wasn't. Ricki was very quiet. She didn't make any moves. All she did was get mad at me because she knew Kay liked me. Ricki did not like me at all."

Ricki wasn't alone in the jealousy department. Dobbie was none too happy about the situation, either. She made her feelings on the subject plain to Dot, but it didn't stop Kay from joining them often at Patrick's Park for drinks and dancing.

Fortunately, Kay wasn't there the night at closing time after a game when a group of emboldened straight couples started making homophobic remarks and harassing Dot, Dobbie, Peanuts, Jessie Glasscock, and their friend, Mary Bynum. The situation escalated to fisticuffs. The combatants took what was now a brawl outside to the parking lot. The bar regulars, all familiar with the gals, took their side. One of the attackers jumped on Mary's back.

"Mary got him down and beat the crap out of him. Dobbie didn't like to fight. She was a big girl, but she just didn't like to fight. So she locked herself in the car and waited until it was all over.

"The next day, we drove back out there, and I found my bracelet in the parking lot where someone had pulled it off my arm in the fight."

Dot told the tale with relish. On the field or off, it wasn't in her nature to back down from a fight.

• • • • • • •

By the end of May 1948, the Ramblers and Queens were deadlocked in their season series, five games apiece. Game eleven was to take place May 27. The *Arizona Republic* previewed the game:

> *The big game of the week for local fans is billed at the Phoenix Softball Park tonight, when the Arizona Brewing Company Queens and PBSW Ramblers renew their high-voltage play in the Girls Major League.*
>
> *As it stands right now, the two clubs have battled to a deadlock in the 10 games thus far—and all 10 have kept the crowds standing until the last out.*

The game was everything it was built up to be—and more. The Ramblers drew first blood with a run in the bottom of the second inning. That lead lasted until the top of the seventh, when the Queens pushed a run across to stave off defeat.

The teams went back and forth, Peralta versus Armstrong, neither pitcher giving an inch and neither squad able to break through. Then came the top of the fourteenth inning.

> *The Ramblers, defending champions of the Amateur Softball Association, were crippled Thursday night when Dot Wilkinson, catcher and captain of the squad, suffered a broken bone just above the ankle.*
>
> *Ford Hoffman, team manager, said yesterday Miss Wilkinson will be lost to the club for at least six weeks.*
>
> *The damaging play came in the 14th inning of the 15-frame heated battle for first place in the Girls Major League which the Queens finally annexed, 3 to 1.*
>
> *Carolyn Morris, regular Queen pitcher, had gone in to pinch-hit for Lois Sauer, right fielder, in the sixth inning and then continued in the game at the right field position. She struck out the first two times at bat and popped to shortstop the third time up, but on her fourth trip she blasted the ball to the fence, rounded third base with what would*

have been the winning run, hesitated, then raced for home. But Miss
Wilkinson was there to take the throw-in, and in the collision at the
plate the Rambler catcher came out with the bone fracture.

    The injury will hinder PBSW's chances in both the Western States
and Phoenix Girls Major League play . . .

Dot, of course, was quick to point out that she caught the ball, made the play, and tagged Morris out to end the threat. For Dot, the rest of the game was a painful experience in every way.

"The worst part about breaking your ankle . . . my manager just took me and put me back on the bench, and he sent to the club room and got a big bucket of ice and put my foot in that. And I had to sit there until the game was over. That hurt a heckuva lot worse than breaking my ankle. After the game, Ford took me to the hospital and they put it in a cast."

Unfortunately, rattled by watching Dot go down, the Ramblers gave away two runs in the fifteenth that sealed the win for the Queens.

The cast ran from Dot's foot to just below the knee. She hobbled around on crutches for weeks, anxious to get back on the field. It was the longest Dot had gone without playing ball since the very first day she stepped on the field with the Ramblers, off-season notwithstanding.

The injury didn't prevent Dot from traveling with the team when they embarked on a swing through Southern California at the beginning of June. The Ramblers swept through Western States Girls Major League opponents Buena Park, Santa Ana, and Monrovia with convincing series wins at each stop.

In one of the early games, the Ramblers were short a player. Rather than forfeit the game, Dot volunteered to take the field, still with her leg encased in plaster. "I couldn't catch on that leg, but I could stand. So I put myself in at center field and everyone ran around me. At least we didn't have to forfeit the game!"

Mostly, Dot watched the games from the bench, cajoling and encouraging her teammates, including backup catcher Zada Boles, as they fought to stay in contention.

At the end of June, one month after Dot's injury, the Ramblers were behind in the series with the Queens, seven games to five.

In Western States Girls Major League play, Fresno was tearing it up. They'd won thirty straight games. The Ramblers desperately tried to keep pace, but they remained two games back going into a six-game series with the Rockets.

Dot was itching to get back into action, despite the fact that she still was more than two weeks away from the target Ford had set for her to return to play. If the Ramblers could win the series with Fresno, they'd move into first place in the league. The night before the series with the Rockets, Dot tested her leg by pinch-hitting in the fifth inning of the losing effort against the Queens. She assured Ford that she was ready to go.

Still, Ford held Dot out for the first games of the series. The Ramblers broke Fresno's thirty-three-game winning streak with a 4–1 victory. The series seesawed back and forth after that, and on July 5, 1948, Dot finally donned her five-finger glove, flimsy chest protector, and mask and got back behind home plate to catch.

The Ramblers triumphed in fifteen grueling innings, giving them the series lead and closing the distance in the Western States Girls Major League standings between the second-place Ramblers and the first-place Rockets. Dot's leg held up and she rarely, if ever, relinquished the mask after that.

· · · · · · ·

The rest of the season progressed without incident. Dot continued to stop by on her way to work to say hello to Kay, and Kay continued to call down to Patrick's Park to see if Dot was there and join her and the gang for drinks and dancing, which continued to irk both Dobbie and Ricki.

Perhaps coincidentally, perhaps not, late in the '48 season, Kay and Ricki committed to leaving Phoenix and the Queens and moving to New Orleans to play for Freda Savona and the Jax for the 1949 season.

Meanwhile, the Ramblers battled back and forth with the Queens for supremacy in the Girls Major League and with the Fresno Rockets in the

Western States Girls Major League. In the latter, the Ramblers and Rockets dueled to a tie. Both teams would head to the world tournament.

On September 7, 1948, the Ramblers and Queens took the field for a doubleheader that would decide not only the season series between the two teams but also the Metropolitan Phoenix Championship. At the time, the Queens were one game ahead in the rivalry with the Ramblers, but the Ramblers had a one-game lead in the Girls Major League overall. If the Queens, who were favored, won the first game of the twin bill, then the series with the Ramblers would belong to them. If they took the second game, the league title would belong to them as well.

Dot and the Ramblers had other plans. In the fifth inning, second baseman Betty Harris tripled. As was her custom, Dot banged the barrel of the bat against her cleats to dislodge the dirt, stepped to the plate, and stared down the pitcher. Then, she smacked an RBI single for the first score of the game. The Ramblers tacked on three more runs in the sixth for all the insurance they needed.

The 4–0 victory clinched the Girls Major League title for the Ramblers. Maybe just as satisfying was the fact that the shutout evened the season series between the Ramblers and the Queens at thirteen games apiece.

The second half of the doubleheader was called after five extra innings with the teams tied at two. It marked the third time the teams had played to a tie that year. Immediately following the game, the Ramblers took off for Portland, Oregon, for the 1948 ASA World Softball Championships.

· · · · · · ·

The Ramblers cruised through the early stages of the tournament, including a 7–1 thrashing of the Louisiana team. Dot was the heroine of that one with a single and a bases-clearing inside-the-park home run. In fact, Dot was on a tear at the plate. The next day, against rival Western States Girls Major League foe Fresno, Dot smashed a triple that brought home Betty Harris. The Ramblers won that contest, 3–0.

That set up a battle of the undefeated between the Ramblers and the hometown favorite Lind and Pomeroy (Portland) Florists team and pitching ace Betty Evans. The winner of this contest would move into the finals. The loser would be dropped into the once-beaten bracket and have to fight their way back or be eliminated from the tournament.

The crowd, 8,124 rowdy, partisan Portland-rooting fans, overflowed the stadium. With the score knotted at zero, Portland finally got to Amy Peralta in the sixth inning. They put across three runs, but the Ramblers weren't finished yet. A pair of Phoenix runners reached base in the seventh with no outs, and it looked as though the Ramblers might blast their way back into the game. Instead, Evans got two Ramblers to whiff and forced a third out on a slow roller to end the threat and the game.

To the delight of the crowd, Portland found itself in the finals. Their opponent would be the survivor of the once-beaten bracket. In the unlikely event Portland lost the next contest, as the only undefeated team in the double-elimination tournament, they still would have another opportunity to win the title.

Fittingly, it was the Ramblers that came roaring back from the brink, and this time Amy shut down Portland, 2–0. The loss leveled the playing field, and now the Ramblers and Portland would play one last game against each other, this time for the right to call themselves world champions.

Dot still had a bitter taste in her mouth from the 1947 ASA fiasco. For a year, everyone had been referring to the Ramblers as the "de facto" champions. She badly wanted to win the championship fair and square and get rid of the asterisk next to the Ramblers' championship designation.

If the crowd had been raucous for the first two games between these two teams, now the stadium was wild. That was fine with Dot. The more animated the setting, the better she liked it.

When Portland's catcher tripled in the second inning and the next batter drew a walk and stole second base, things looked bleak for the Ramblers. But with Dot calling the pitches, Amy calmly dialed in on Dot's glove and forced the next three batters to pop the ball up, ending the threat.

In the top of the fifth, the Ramblers pushed across three runs, with Dobbie leading the way. She had three of the Ramblers' seven hits in the game. The final score was Phoenix three, Portland zero.

Finally, after an eight-year drought, the Ramblers once again were the rightful world champions. Dot received All-American honors and another trophy to add to her burgeoning collection.

A week later, the three most prominent leaders in softball got together to compile a squad comprised of the best of the best. The headline in the *Arizona Republic* announced: ALL-TIME ALL AMERICA SOFTBALL GIRLS TEAM SELECTED BY PILOTS.

The article was penned by columnist Arnott Duncan, who'd regularly been following the women's softball circuit for the newspaper.

> An all-time All-America girls' softball team said to be the best ever picked was selected by managers of three of the outstanding teams in the sport's history. . . .
>
> Ford Hoffman, pilot of the PBSW Ramblers, Amateur Softball champions for the past two years; Freda Savona, manager of the Jax Brewers of New Orleans, five times ASA crown bearers and winners of the 1948 NSC tourney, and Larry Walker, head of the A-1 Queens, last year's NSC champs and runners-up to the Jax this year, haggled in a friendly manner over their selections and came up with what Hoffman called the best all-time All-America ever put together.
>
> Six players were unanimous choices—Amy Peralta of the Ramblers and Nina Korgan of the Jax, pitchers; Dottie Wilkinson of the Ramblers, catcher; Kay Rich of Fresno, California, first base; Olympia Savona, Jax, third base; and Virginia (Dobbie) Dobson, Ramblers, outfield.

"Ford never told me those kinds of things. I never knew how many All-American honors I had; I never knew any of that. I just wanted to play ball. Once, I overheard one of the girls complaining to Ford that I thought an awful lot of myself. She said, 'Dot is so full of herself. It's like she thinks she's the best.'

"Ford answered her, 'She is.' But he never said that *to* me, only *about* me. Probably just as well."

1948 PBSW Ramblers official championship team photo. Top row, from left to right: Manager Ford Hoffman, Amelina Peralta, Jessie Glasscock, unknown, Margie Law, Virginia "Dobbie" Dobson, Delores Low, Mary Irwin, Luella Reese. Bottom row, from left to right: Betty Harris, Zada Boles, Dot Wilkinson, Jean Hutsell, Marie Rogers, Nadine Moody, and Kathleen "Peanuts" Eldridge. *Courtesy of the Dot Wilkinson Collection*

Several days later, the state of Arizona and the city of Phoenix threw a parade and a dinner.

> *The parade will end at the state capitol and speaker of the house will present the trophy to the winners.*
>
> *Forming at Central Avenue and Roosevelt at 10:30 a.m., the parade will move south to Washington and thence to the capitol. The team members, who defended their 1947 title successfully, will ride in open cars donated for the occasion by car dealers. A string quartet will go along in a truck . . .*

The dinner was held at the Westward Ho that night. It was open to the public, and two hundred Ramblers fans turned out to mark the occasion. As always, Dot's very proud parents were on hand to help her celebrate.

"My parents came to every local game," Dot said. "My dad was too nervous to sit and watch, so he would jump up and spend most of the game at the concession stand drinking a beer. When he'd hear a cheer, why, he'd check it out.

"My mom had so much trouble with her eyesight that eventually she became legally blind. Yet, she 'saw' everything that happened on the field. When I would ask her how she knew what happened on a particular play, she would tell me she had the person next to her describe it to her." Dot said this with great pride, the same kind of pride her folks took in her.

· · · · · · ·

Dot's older sister, Ruth; her father, Allan; mother, Alice; and Dot circa the 1940s. *Courtesy of the Dot Wilkinson Collection*

By 1949, Ford had schooled Dot in all the ins and outs of his real estate business. He encouraged her to get her own real estate license, which she did. For the next step in her education, Ford brought Dot in as a partner in several of his real estate purchases. He taught her how to spot worthwhile properties and how to turn them for a profit.

Then Dot got the idea to include Dobbie in some of her real estate deals. "I don't know whether she ever gave me any money or not. We were going together, and I was just trying to get her involved.

"I used to get the properties for practically nothing. We probably paid monthly payments on them. Things like that would come up to the real estate office and I couldn't do it myself."

So, together, Dot and Dobbie first bought three lots that they resold for a profit. And then they purchased six more properties. Dot's real estate career was taking off.

Meanwhile, her star had fully risen in the softball world. Newspapers and magazines ran large-scale features on her. *Arizona Highways* magazine ran a front-page story titled Arizona's Larruping Lassies, a full-color, multipage, comprehensive examination of the women's softball scene in Phoenix, the stars of the game, and the three major hometown teams—the Ramblers, the Queens, and the Maids.

Of Dot, writer Jerry McLain said:

> *Mention the Ramblers, and the names of Dottie Wilkinson and Amy Peralta inevitably bob up. They began this season, their 13th year as battery mates, and the peppery little Wilkinson is managing the Ramblers.*
>
> *Now regarded as one of the greatest feminine catchers in the business, Miss Wilkinson carries a .340 lifetime batting average and is a Gibraltar on defense. She has been an All-American six times and has participated in 13 national tournaments . . .*

A headline in the March 21, 1949, *Arizona Republic* newspaper boasted, Dottie Wilkinson, PBSW Rambler Ace, Rated One of Softball's Best. The feature sports a publicity photo of Dot bunting. The picture takes up the bulk of the page.

Naturally, Dot did not disappoint. Her play in 1949 lived up to all the hype, as did the Ramblers. Although the competition had stiffened considerably in the Western States Girls Major League, the Ramblers again emerged on top.

The official ceremony opening the 1949 World Softball Championships in Portland, Oregon. That's the PBSW Ramblers standing along the third baseline. Dot is closest to home plate. *Courtesy of the Dot Wilkinson Collection via USA Softball*

At the world championship—held separately from the men's tournament for the first time—Dot and a few of her teammates kept a secret. Ramblers All-American pitcher/outfielder Margie Law was six months pregnant with her second child.

"I didn't know she was that far along. I knew she was pregnant. A bunch of us Ramblers got an apartment together in Portland so that we could keep an eye on Margie. Every morning she had morning sickness. We'd be cooking breakfast, and she'd be feeling like she needed to go throw up. It happened before every game. But she went out there and played anyway."

In the early rounds, the Ramblers seemed unstoppable. They plowed over their first three opponents without breaking a sweat. Then came the semifinal nailbiter with the Peoria Dieselettes. The outcome was all the more remarkable for Margie's condition.

Dieselettes' pitcher Marie Wadlow described the scene:

At Portland, the Dieselettes finished fourth, beating Orange, 2–0, then being knocked into the loser's bracket by Phoenix, 1–0. I guess that was the wildest and most heartbreaking loss of my career. Pitching a two-hitter against the Ramblers, with 11 strikeouts (the Dieselettes had four hits off Amy Peralta and eight strikeouts), the score was 0–0 going into the last of the 7th inning.

There was one out with Margie Law on third base for the Ramblers.

A fly ball was hit to left field. Margie tagged up and headed for home. The throw from Dieselette left fielder Carolyn Thome was well ahead of Margie, so Margie turned around and headed back to third. However, the throw from Carolyn went over the head of the catcher, so the third base coach waved Margie back to home. There was a short backstop, though, so the Dieselette first baseman, Lillian Goll, who was backing up the play, picked up the ball and started chasing Margie back to third. Lillian's throw to third was high and sailed into left field. Margie turned once again and headed back to home. Carolyn's throw again was ahead of Margie—Margie headed back to third.

The throw went over the catcher's head again! The Dieselette catcher, Marian Kneer, shagged the ball and flipped it to me on Homeplate [sic]. I guess I REALLY had the plate blocked, because just as I caught the ball and turned to tag Margie—POWIE!!

Margie hit me like a ton of bricks, I dropped the ball, and Margie scored the winning run! It took several minutes to revive me, and after I found out what had happened, I wished that they had left me in the blissful state of unconsciousness!!

The shutout win over the Dieselettes set up the championship final; once again the Ramblers would be pitted against the hometown favorite Portland team. This time, however, it was Portland that was coming out of the losers' bracket to face the undefeated Ramblers, not the other way around.

The Portland players were exhausted, having played three games in one day the day before, two of them extra-inning contests, just for the right to face the Ramblers in the final.

Amy pitched the first six innings of the game. In the sixth, with the score 2–0 Ramblers, the first run of the tournament scored by an opponent against the Ramblers crossed the plate; the run was unearned. With the score 2–1, Margie came in from left field and relieved Amy. She shut down Portland the rest of the way, and the Ramblers were repeat champions—their third world championship of the decade. Dot and her teammates celebrated with unbridled joy.

17

Three and Out

THE THREE-TIME WORLD CHAMPION PBSW Ramblers prided themselves on being a homegrown, Arizona-born-and-bred team; the nucleus of the squad had been in place for many years. That is part of what makes their consistent success at the highest levels of the game so very remarkable.

While other teams like the Queens, the Maids, and the Jax regularly cycled through players, importing the best talent from all over the country, the Ramblers stayed true to their founding principles.

Fortunately for them, Arizona was the softball capital of the nation. So it should've been no surprise when Ford "discovered" a young Black teenager from Tucson with so much raw talent he couldn't wait to see what she could do in the Ramblers' lineup.

However, in 1950, the color barrier was alive and well throughout the nation, Jackie Robinson's 1947 arrival in Brooklyn to play with the Dodgers notwithstanding. The addition of southpaw Billie Harris on the Ramblers would not come without risk. Ford and Dot decided to introduce Billie to the fans slowly.

In her inaugural season with the team, Billie often played with the Ramblers' farm team, the Dudettes. Billie primarily was a pitcher, but with Margie and Amy still carrying the load for the Ramblers at that position, Dot slotted Billie into select Ramblers games in right field.

"Billie was lightning fast," Dot recollected. "She wasn't a hard hitter, but she ran like the wind. I suppose she would've been the precursor to today's slap hitters. She could beat out just about any ball she got her bat on, including infield grounders.

"To get her into the games, we'd put her in right field. But Billie never threw overhand, so she'd whip the ball in from the outfield underhanded. She's the only player I ever saw do that."

Billie would not make her pitching debut for the Ramblers until June 6, 1954, against a Ricki Caito–led California team named the Top Hats.

Also in 1950, Dot, Ford, and the rest of the team grew weary of playing all their "home" games in ballparks that weren't home at all.

"We got tired of playing out at the Phoenix Softball Park and being second fiddle to the Queens, because that was the Queens' home park. So Ford just said, 'Let's get together and build a family ballpark.' And that's what we did.

"Ford and I had some properties together, and we sold the mortgages to a guy named Sergeant who had a lot of money and we got the money from him to build the park.

"The land for Rambler Field belonged to a couple that owned the motel on Van Buren. They had the property all the way from Van Buren to Washington. The first part of the property was 3600 Van Buren. The couple had the motel there and they lived there. The back side, at 3700 East Washington Street, they let us have to put the whole park in, just for paying the taxes, which was not very much. They were fans and they were helping us, and they did until the very end.

"When we first secured the property, we brought in all the girls from the team. We hauled manure, and we planted the grass, and the girls helped build that whole field and fix it all right to plant the grass. Margie's dad built all the stands. And then later we built the restrooms underneath for the fans.

Members of the Ramblers all pitched in to construct Rambler Field, which opened in Phoenix in August 1950. *Courtesy of the Dot Wilkinson Collection*

"We had a men's room and a girls' room and then we had our locker room where we had showers. Later we built our club room. We had that the last few years. We built it so that we would have a place to have fun after the games without having to go out anywhere. We had a refrigerator there and if they had leftover food in the concession, they'd bring it up there. We let people put a dollar in a jug for beer or whatever. If they didn't have a dollar then they didn't have to . . . if they wanted a beer, we took care of it for them. It was just a place to hang out.

"Sometimes we'd take the other teams down there, but most of the time it was just our team. We had pictures of the players on the walls and a place to dance. Many times we'd stay there until two or three o'clock in the morning. Ricki and I, sometimes we'd be going home, and we'd go close up the concession stand and get up the money and all the ticket office receipts and do all that and throw the money bag in the back of the car and then go party. We didn't have to worry about things back then.

"We built everything on there just out of whatever we could get. I don't know where the money came from. Ford got a lot of the stuff donated and different things. He got the lights from somewhere and we moved them to Rambler Field. I think the lights were from the old Municipal Stadium; he made a deal for them.

"The stadium held three thousand people. We had a big bleacher on the one side and a small bleacher on the other side, and they were all right up against the fence. And then we had two hundred box seats in a little square place, down on the ground on the first base side. Ford bought those chairs; I think they were theater seats. There's something we had for part of the first two rows and then the others were just regular metal chairs. It wasn't fancy, but it was just in a good area. They were all fifty-cent general admission seats. Box seats probably cost a dollar. Those box seats were the only assigned seats. Everything else was first come, first served.

"Margie Law's dad put up all the bleachers, and that's all the stadium was. We put up the fences on the inside later so we could sell advertising all the way around for a couple hundred dollars a year, which helped us.

"I sold a lot of the ads. We got the advertising from the suppliers for the concession stand. I convinced them if we were going to sell their beer, we needed their sign on the fence. That's how we did it.

"That helped us out once we had the fence up all the way around. We had signs on all of it. Along with the advertising on the fence, we sold programs, and we made money out of the concession stand. The concession stand paid a lot of the freight.

"We bought the supplies from a warehouse, and two of the girls, Marge Lange and Sue Reilly, ran the concession as volunteers. They made it like a restaurant—hot dogs, chili dogs, cheeseburgers . . .

"We had to get enough money out of the admission prices to pay the other team. They got $150 a game, I think, to start with, and $200 for a doubleheader. So we had to scrounge to come up with that. We had to pay the umpires, one behind home plate and the other in the infield somewhere. I think we paid them something like $17 a game.

"The whole thing was made and run by the team. The only people we ever paid were Kay's father, Daddy Rohrer, who did the groundskeeping, and the umpires.

"We had an old car that we used to drag the field with. It was my old 1932 Chevy that I donated. Daddy Rohrer used to drive it around there. We had an all-dirt infield and a grass outfield. We built the park on the dimensions of what we had. It was 250 feet in center and left. We had to keep all the front of it for parking, but we needed some of the back side of it too.

"That's why right field was so short. It was like 185 feet in right field [from home plate to the fence]. So, we made that fence a lot taller. You had to be a pretty good hitter to get it over that fence. Everybody said it was Wilkinson's Garden, and I did hit some home runs. The distance was fairly short for me to right. But I didn't hit as many homers as Sis King, and Marlene Wells would hit one once in a while.

"Not many people hit home runs then. We had wooden bats and a ball that was not hard and didn't go like the ones they have now. Today's game, with those lightweight aluminum bats and rock-hard balls, well, you hardly have to tap the ball to hit it hard."

Rambler Field would open at the end of August 1950. In the meantime, the regular season featured its share of physical fights between the Ramblers and the Queens and maneuvering and bad blood off the field between the Ramblers, Queens, and a new, different third contestant in the closed Phoenix Women's Major Softball League, the Funk Gems.

The Gems, sponsored by local softball scion Art Funk, were to be managed by none other than Kay Rohrer, who returned to Phoenix for good from New Orleans, minus Ricki, for the 1950 season. Even when she'd been in New Orleans the previous year, Kay had continued to keep in touch with Dot via the telephone.

Ricki, for her part, went back to playing professional ball for Parichy's Bloomer Girls in Chicago.

"Kay and Ricki were together, I guess, one year in Chicago when they were playing ball there in 1947, and then they were together in '48. They played one year here for the Queens, and then they went to New Orleans and they were there. But I have a feeling they'd already decided they weren't going to be together. I don't know. I used to get calls from Kay down there. Of course, Ricki got mad about that too. So they were still together when they were in New Orleans.

"They both left New Orleans, and Ricki went to Chicago with Willie Turner. And I think Willie Turner's mother drove the two of them to Chicago and Kay came here.

"This guy named Jones owned a sporting goods store next to the Fox Phoenix Theatre downtown, and Kay worked for him there. I know that's where I got those shoes that I still have, handmade, and she got me those boots. She kept me in trouble all the time because she always kept giving me stuff and I couldn't explain it.

"I couldn't tell Dobbie where the hell I got them. Dobbie knew I didn't have enough money to buy those things. So I kept them hidden most of the time.

"Anyhow, Kay worked for Jones Western Wear, right on the corner of First or Second Street, right downtown next to the Fox Theatre. I think that Jones got Kay a job at the capitol. And that's when she went to work out there for the tax commission, because I know long before I went with her, I used to go pick her up out there.

"Kay started two teams of her own. She had the Mesa Premiums and the Funk Gems. One of them, the Gems, won the NSC Championship in 1950—they beat the Queens. I don't know how she did it.

"Kay brought in a lot of ballplayers from New Orleans. She brought them in from everywhere. I don't know how she did it, where she got the money . . . . I never asked. But somehow, she did it."

In fact, Kay poached top talent away from the Queens, the Jax, and the now defunct Maids. Included in her Gems lineup were all-star pitcher Carolyn Morris and power-hitting shortstop Merle Keagle. Those acquisitions didn't sit well with Queens manager Larry Walker, who insisted that new, more restrictive rules be put in place preventing one team from raiding another for players.

In addition to the strengthened competition locally, the Ramblers faced upgraded talent in the Western States Girls Major League from the Buena Park Lynx, Fresno, Montebello (California), Portland, and Salt

Lake City. In the end, the Ramblers barely held off the Lynx for the Western States Girls Major League title.

And, as three-time world champions, the Ramblers were the team to beat in San Antonio, site of the 1950 World Softball Championships.

The ascendant Orange Lionettes and star pitcher Bertha Ragan stood directly in the Ramblers' path to retaining their crown. Ragan threw a no-hitter, as the Lionettes ran over the Ramblers in convincing 5–0 fashion, pushing Phoenix into the losers' bracket. That set up a record-setting tournament Saturday to remember, beginning with a seventeen-inning marathon against the Dieselettes in the one-hundred-degree Texas heat. The Ramblers eventually prevailed, 1–0, setting up another showdown with Orange for the championship. To take the title, Phoenix would have to win two consecutive games from Bertha Ragan.

In an eleven-inning thriller, the Ramblers held off the Lionettes, 1–0, to force a winner-take-all, late-night, one-last-game-to-decide-the-championship contest.

Four and a half hours and fifteen long innings after the game began, it ended with the Ramblers finally running out of steam. Orange scored a 3–1 victory in the wee hours of the morning to emerge as the new ASA world champions.

"That was down in San Antonio, Texas [1950]. I caught forty-three innings in that one day. We played against Peoria, Illinois, in the afternoon. We started at two o'clock. We played all afternoon. We played seventeen innings before we finally won. Then we went to the hotel and we changed uniforms.

"We were coming out of the losers' bracket. The Orange Lionettes were in the winners' bracket. So, we played Orange the first game, and we beat them in eleven innings. So we had to play another game, and I think the next game was fifteen or something. It was forty-three all together that I caught. Forty-three innings in one day—and part of it was in the hot sun—and it was hot down there anyway. I think I'm still feeling those innings in my ankles today."

Throughout the 1940s and 1950s, crowds jammed into Phoenix ballparks to watch the women play. Most games were sold out. *Courtesy of the Herb and Dorothy McLaughlin Collection, Greater Arizona Collection, Arizona State University Library*

Part Six

ROUNDING THIRD

18

The Winds of Change
Are Blowing

IT WAS ALMOST AS IF that 1950 tournament took something essential out of Dot and the team. From that moment forward, the Ramblers continued to play at the highest levels of the game, but never again could they break through and win that final game of the championship.

If possible, Dot saw the ball even better in her thirties than she did when she was younger. Her batting averages continued to place her among the best hitters in the game, she amassed more All-American honors than any player in history (nineteen—a record that still stands today), and her prowess behind the plate was unmatched by any catcher ever in the game of women's softball.

Her reputation for being a fierce competitor—a hard-nosed, never-back-down, never-quit player and team leader—earned her both the enmity and respect of players and managers everywhere, just as it had done from the very outset. Still, as good as she was, the competition continued to get tougher, as evinced particularly by the teams from California.

The Orange Lionettes three-peated as champions, adding titles in '51 and '52, before the Fresno Rockets knocked them off their perch in '53 and

'54. Orange wrested the title back in '55 and '56, and the Rockets took it back again in '57. Thereafter, the Lionettes and an upstart team from Connecticut, the Brakettes, virtually monopolized the ASA championships.

Still, the Ramblers consistently finished in close contention for the title. Fans packed the stands at Rambler Field and everywhere the team played. They remained the best softball show around.

The addition of Billie to the team meant some adjustments. In many places the Ramblers played in the 1950s, segregation ruled the day, and Billie put up with plenty of bigotry.

"One time, we were in Salt Lake City. The team went out to eat after the game. When we got to the restaurant, Billie went straight to the bathroom. We all ordered steaks and when the waiter came back to the table the next time, Billie was at the table. The waiter said they didn't serve 'colored' folks. Ford told the manager, 'If you don't serve Billie, we won't eat here.' Well, the steaks were already cooked. Ford didn't care. We all got up and walked out.

Members of the 1954 Ramblers. From left to right: Dot Wilkinson, unknown, Kay Rohrer, Bonnie Johns, and Virginia "Dobbie" Dobson.
Courtesy of the Dot Wilkinson Collection

"There were other times when Billie would have to stay somewhere other than the motel where the rest of the team was staying, or she would have to eat outside. It was terrible. It was hard. But we all stuck together. We were a team."

Billie's presence wasn't the only dynamic shift on the Ramblers, either. In 1954, after sitting out from professional competition the requisite year to regain her amateur status, Kay Rohrer joined the Ramblers as a shortstop and first baseman. Naturally, that didn't go over too well with Dobbie.

As it turned out, Dobbie's instincts about Kay's intentions might have been correct. "My bedroom was on the first floor facing the street," Dot said. "One night, Kay tried to climb in through my bedroom window. She thought better of it when she realized Dobbie was there with me. Dobbie wasn't any too happy about that. We had a big fight over it."

Kay wasn't the only point of contention in Dot and Dobbie's relationship. "Dobbie's mother was always suspicious of us. She caught us one time fooling around on the couch. She knew. She called Dobbie a 'woman-lover.'

"Dobbie was their only daughter, and her mother wanted grandkids. So she wanted her daughter to get married, and she won out. She won the race.

"Her mother was pushing Dobbie to date men all the time. Her mother tried to get her to go with the guy that lived next door. I can't remember his name. In fact, she did go out with him a couple of times to keep her mother happy, because she was on her all the time about that. So it made it difficult. But Dobbie was able to shake that guy off, and I thought that was the end of it.

"Dobbie and I had been going to the 902 [bar] for quite some time, and her folks used to go to the 902. They liked to go anywhere where they could drink.

"We met this other guy, Dub, at the bar, and he had a friend named Dick. They both worked for the power company. One night at the bar, Dub and Dick talked us into going quail hunting with them. We kind of did that just to silence the conversation with Dobbie's mother. Then

Dobbie started going out with Dub on Friday nights just to ease the pain at home.

"So I'd go out with Dick. I enjoyed him because he liked to dance and so did I. So we got decked out and we'd go somewhere where we could dance. But he got serious about me. And so I put a stop to it. I ended it. I said, 'Dick, this is not going to work.' I didn't tell him why, but I told him I didn't want it anymore."

Meanwhile, Dobbie was making a different choice. "I knew it. I knew something was up because she started going out with Dub more often. . . . We argued about it quite a bit. I hadn't even thought that she would want to get married. That didn't enter my mind."

On June 2, 1955, a little more than two months after the ink dried on Green Webster "Dub" Bickle's divorce decree and while Dot and Dobbie were still together, Dobbie's parents whisked her and Dub off to get them married.

"Evidently, she told her mother and dad when they talked her into going and getting married, she said, 'I told them I have to be back. I gotta play ball tonight.' And she did. She got back in time for the game and that's when she told me, I guess after the game. I can't remember whether she told me or she told Ford and he might've told me."

When Dobbie married Dub, Dot took the six properties she and Dobbie had purchased together and split them evenly. "I deeded three of them to Dobbie and I kept three. She used those as a down payment when she and Dub bought their first house.

"I told her one time, I said, 'You broke my heart when you went off and married Dub.' She said, 'I know.' And I think that was it. She was sorry the rest of her life. It wasn't easy 'cause she still played ball for the Ramblers for another season after that.

"I thought she cared about Dub, because she acted like it. They got married and had two boys . . . until I talked to her way later on, after Dub died and Dobbie was alone, and I'd take her out to lunch because she wanted to go.

"I'd say, 'How come you were not happy? You got married. He was a good guy, and you had two sons. I know you had a problem, because the one son got killed in an automobile accident. I know that, but why weren't you happy?'

"[I knew she was unhappy] because she used to call me in the middle of the night. A lot of times she and Dub were drinking after they got married. When she got to drinking, then it came out, and she would tell me, 'It's because I forgot to fall out of love with you, Dot.'"

• • • • • • •

Predictably, Dot wasn't alone for long. Kay, who had been less than subtly waiting in the wings, eagerly stepped into the void.

"Kay was still working at the capitol in 1955, and we still went out to lunch. She'd come by the house early in the morning and stop and say hello. In 1956, she just moved in with me in the house on Twenty-First Avenue."

As she'd done previously with Dobbie, Dot included Kay in her real estate investments. But, unlike with Dobbie, Kay was an equal partner.

Dot and Kay Rohrer, 1950s Ramblers. *Courtesy of the Dot Wilkinson Collection*

"Kenny Wall was a salesman in the office, and I was working there. That was when they were putting up the freeway out on the West Side for I-17, I guess it was, or I-10. I don't know. And they were tearing houses down, and Kenny and I bought five or six houses together and moved them somewhere and put them in different places. You could buy them cheap because they had to be moved. That's how I got in partnership with Kenny. We moved those onto Gibson Lane, I think, for some of them.

"When Kay got involved, she borrowed twenty-five hundred bucks from her brother, who was in the service, and bought Kenny out. From then on, I was partners with Kay instead of Kenny. And then, after that, I started getting more properties with Kay.

"We didn't fix them up. We had certain things, of course, we had to fix. We had to put in hot-water tanks, etcetera. When you move a house, you have to fix it so it's livable. But we did not do that ourselves.

"Personally, I did not get into flipping houses until later, when I was with Ricki. I made arrangements to get it done and that type of thing. And we had guys working at the office that did that work."

Dot and Kay found other ventures to invest in as well. "On some properties, Hoffman Realty had sold them to somebody and they came back because they couldn't make the payments. Some of those I would put in Kay's name. That's how we made a fortune on one of them. We bought a lot back that somebody had bought for a reason and then let it go. And it came back in through the office and I took it and put it in Kay's name alone. A guy bought it that I think was in the photography business. He put a big business on it. It was an acre. And I think we got close to $100,000 for something that we bought for probably hundreds."

Despite Dot and Kay's burgeoning romance and business successes, all was not well. Kay, whose grandmother and mother had passed away very young from breast cancer, got her diagnosis shortly before she moved in with Dot and Dot's folks. Before her suitcases were even unpacked, Kay underwent a successful mastectomy. At the time, she was thirty-three years old.

When she recovered from the surgery, Kay became restless. The house on Twenty-First Avenue felt small and confining. She wanted them to move.

"We went to visit my sister, Ruth, on St. Charles. They lived at 39 East St. Charles Street. This house at 25 East St. Charles had a FOR SALE sign on it. And Kay says, 'Let's go look at that house.' So, we went up and looked at it and I bought it in my name. This was 1957.

"I just went down and talked to the guy—he was a sheep man. And I just made arrangements to buy it on terms because I'm sure we didn't have any money. I probably have the contract where I paid so much down and paid them so much a month. Because at that time, they were related to the people next door, I think. And so that's how we bought that house and paid for it.

"After Kay and I bought that house, we built a pool in the back. The property had two lots. We built the pool on part of the second lot. My folks were in the house at that time when we first bought that house. We had three bedrooms. One was mine and Kay's, and one was my mother's, and one was my dad's.

"My folks never asked why Kay and I shared a bedroom. They loved Kay, like they loved Peanuts and Dobbie. My girlfriends were all family."

"The house that I had bought from the sheep people had a big garage. My brother-in-law, Joe, and I had a checking account that we'd made special to build a house for my folks on that piece of the property. He and Kay were working out there all the time. They built my folks a beautiful place. It had a large living room and a nice kitchen and a bathroom that was all tiled, and they had a big bedroom."

• • • • • • •

With the housing situation settled, Dot had other delicate issues to tend to. By 1956–57, Ford was a changed man, and it wasn't for the better. According to Dot, Ford got involved in an extramarital affair. Dot was not shy about telling Ford her opinion of his choices.

"They started going out and they'd go to the bars and end up going to motels. I'd get bills because I took care of the finances in the office, and I was very hurt about it. I talked to Ford about it and told him he was making a bad mistake.

"We talked about it, and he knew it. Because this woman talked him into going to the bars and they'd play pool and do all this kind of stuff and be seen. That's not Ford Hoffman. Whenever we went out after a ball game, sometimes the girls would have a beer. Ford never, ever did. He was a drinker, but I never saw him take a drink in my whole life. He was just always like a father to me.

"This woman went through his money."

Ford divorced his wife, Peggy, and married the other woman.

"He was selling his mortgages at big discounts. I didn't have a lot of money then, but I had some. I told him 'If you're going to give these away, I'm going to buy some of them.' So I bought a couple, three from him."

The entire episode was the beginning of a lengthy estrangement between Dot and Ford.

• • • • • • •

But first, Dot and Ford would have to manage their way through the 1957 season. As always, the Ramblers made short work of the competition on the field. They arrived in Buena Park, California, for the twenty-fifth World Softball Championships as one of the prohibitive favorites.

That was before they drew the Orange Lionettes as their first-round opponent. Ricki, having left Chicago for her native California several years before, was now the star second baseman for the Lionettes. Bertha Ragan, the former Orange pitching great, had hitched her star to the up-and-coming Raybestos Brakettes, so Ricki brought in ace Teddy Hamilton, a pitcher from her previous team.

Amy Peralta had retired from the Ramblers by then, and Alma Wilson, formerly of Toronto, had joined Margie Law as a regular in the Phoenix pitching rotation. Wilson drew the assignment to pitch that initial game.

Orange struck first, scoring two runs in the second inning, but the Ramblers countered to tie the game in the third. The score remained knotted at two until the first extra inning, when Ricki singled, advanced to second on a sacrifice, and scored on a single, giving the victory to Orange.

Dot takes a throw at the plate to nab the Orange Lionettes' Dorothy "Snookie" (Harrell) Doyle during a 1956 game. *Courtesy of the Dot Wilkinson Collection via Carol Spanks/Orange Lionettes*

The loss knocked Dot and the Ramblers into the losers' bracket. The road to the championship would require Phoenix to win seven consecutive games to reach the final.

First, they plowed over the team from Springfield, Ohio. Then, the next day, Alma threw a no-hit, no-run gem in the afternoon against Minneapolis. That night, Margie pitched a perfect game, striking out fifteen St. Louis batters and leading the Ramblers to a 5–0 rout.

The next two victims were Portland and Denver. Those wins set up a dramatic rematch with Orange. Once again, the Lionettes drew first blood, and the Ramblers scrambled back to tie the game in the fifth. Also as before, the contest went an extra inning.

This time, Dot doubled, went to third on Kay Rohrer's bunt single, and scored the game-winning run, the one that knocked Ricki and Orange out of the tournament, on another single.

Next, the Ramblers dispensed with Huntington Park, setting up a final with the unbeaten Fresno Rockets and their star shortstop, Kay Rich.

Unfortunately for the Ramblers, the Rockets' pitcher, Ginny Busick, was pitching some of her best ball of the tournament. More consequential for Dot and the Ramblers: Dot lost her temper while contesting a call and got tossed out of the game by the umpire.

Famed women's softball historian Stormy Irwin was in the stands for that last game. She chronicled what she witnessed in a 1963 edition of her widely distributed newsletter:

"I'd never seen women play softball like they did that night. The players were so talented I could hardly believe it all. I had another surprise . . . the catcher from the Arizona team (called the Desert Warhorse) was unhappy over a call by the referee and *she let him know it*!! He stepped back and pointed to the bleachers, sending the catcher (Dot Wilkinson) to that area. After the game, the referees all left the park through a gate which was next to the bleachers where Dot sat. She climbed down and tossed a glass of water in his face as he left!!! I was aghast!! I had NEVER seen that happen before."

In the end, Busick pitched a two-hit masterpiece that once again left Phoenix second best.

Several days after they returned to Phoenix, Dot received an official letter from Ford. It was addressed to her, Margie, and Dobbie:

Dear Friends:

This will serve as my resignation from any relationship with Rambler Field either as part owner, operator, lessee. This letter is your notice that I will cancel my interest back to you all at no cost.

My decision is based on what is best for Rambler Field and personal reasons I cannot publicize at this time.

I shall resign my team capacity to Mr. Peterson at PBSW with the recommendation they continue, with your group recommending new management to them.

Both Rambler Field and PBSW have my 100% good will and wishes for future success. It is a life time thrill to have been associated with the "Best."

Very sincerely,

Ford Hoffman

"He didn't say that much in the letter, but I know why he resigned. He didn't want to embarrass the team. He didn't want the public to know that he was still involved with the Ramblers because he was not proud of what he was doing.

"I wished I had been able to tell him how much I appreciated what he did for me. I didn't, because he went off with that woman and messed himself up and started drinking and kind of blew it. I know it ruined his life, because he cared more about that team than anything and that woman just ruined it. That was it.

"Ford was good about organizing things. If he'd made up his mind he wanted to do something, he just did it. When I think about how he arranged for us to go to all those different ballparks all over the world and that we made it every year . . . . We had to work at it.

"We sold a lot of tickets and did a lot of things, but he made it so we could buy gas and pay for hotels, and he did all that. Ford was an amazing guy, way ahead of his time.

"He loved the Ramblers. He named them. He started them. He just did everything for them. And he did the same for me. He did everything for me. And I didn't even know that till I had grown up and he's gone. I really wouldn't have what I have today if it hadn't been for him. And I know that.

"I cared about Ford, and he cared about me, and he cared about all the girls. Louise Miller, he sent her to college. She graduated from ASU, and several of the girls did."

With Ford's resignation, Dot took complete control of and responsibility for her beloved Ramblers.

"When I first took over the team, I found out that he was paying for several of the girls to go to college. So, I kept on paying for him—not me personally—but I arranged to get it through Rambler Field or something. Whatever he was doing, I tried to keep doing it. Ford taught me how to be a good athlete, a good businessperson, and a good person. He taught me to do the right thing."

Shortly after Ford's resignation, Margie Law retired from the Ramblers.

Taking over complete control of the Ramblers improved neither Dot's reputation for pugnacity nor her disposition. National Softball Hall of Famer Carol Spanks, who joined the Orange Lionettes in 1958, played for the Buena Park Lynx prior to that. She learned the hard way about Dot's tenacity behind the plate.

"I was maybe seventeen or eighteen years old. My manager coached me about Dot the first time I played against her. He told me not to slide into her but to try to move her off the plate. So, there I was at third base, heading for home. I thought, 'I'll just run over her and knock her on her ass.' She lowered her shoulder and lifted me. The next thing I knew, she'd launched me clear into the backstop. She looked at me and said, 'Don't ever do that again.' I never did.

"I don't ever remember Dot sliding. She'd just come in standing up and dare you. She was just a hard-nosed ballplayer, always in the umpire's face, swearing and yelling. She argued—a lot.

"Orange hosted the championship in 1954. We had dugouts you stepped down into. There were Cokes sitting around in bottles. Dot got hot at one of the umpires, took one of those Cokes, fizzed it up, and sprayed it at him. She got kicked out of the game."

Spanks also had a ringside seat to some of the more heated encounters on the field between Dot and Ricki.

"We were playing the Ramblers, and Ricki, of course, was playing second base. Dot got a big hit—it ended up being a triple. I'm not sure what happened as Dot was running toward second . . . maybe she said something to Ricki when she passed her. All I know is, the next thing, Ricki was chasing Dot and jumped on her back. Dot carried her all the way to third base. I'd be very surprised if Caito wasn't ejected for that stunt, but I don't recall."

Dot corroborated Carol's recollection: "I said, 'Goddamn it, Caito, get off my back.' We were not friends, and we were friends, but not."

Carol threw her head back and laughed. "Those two were always at each other during games. I remember another time, Ricki was coming around third, heading for home. Dot made the play at home and was ready to throw the ball elsewhere. Ricki rolled over to come up between Dot's legs on all fours to disrupt the throw. Dot said something like, 'I'll kill you if you do that. Ricki just rolled away. After a while, I even asked Ricki if she was calling Dot and setting these kinds of antics up in advance because they happened so frequently."

19

The Pain of Loss

IN OCTOBER 1958, DOT turned thirty-seven. Three days later, she, Kay, and a few others were outside in the backyard at the St. Charles house, doing some home improvements.

"A bunch of the girls and Kay's brother were helping us put up the grape stake fence around the pool we'd built," Dot remembered. "I asked Kay where my dad was. Mother said he hadn't gotten up that morning. They slept in different twin beds, and mother was blind.

"Mom got up early and came over and had breakfast with us and was in the house with us. Kay and I got worried, so she went into Mother and Dad's house to see where he was. That's when she found him.

"He wasn't breathing, so Kay ran over and got her brother and had him come over. My dad had just gone to sleep. He was lying there peacefully with his hands behind his head. He'd passed away.

"I'd been worried because the day before that, he'd had a cough. I had gone down and bought him some cough medicine and I thought, *My God, he probably took it all.* But the truth was, he never even touched it. So that wasn't what it was.

"He was sick. He had told me several days before that he had been in some kind of cold air. He used to walk from St. Charles down Central on the other side of Southern [Avenue] to that bar down there every day. It was the White Horse or something at that time. That day, he said he got tired on the walk. When my dad was too tired to walk and have his beer, I knew he was in trouble."

Dot's father was laid to rest on October 15, 1958. He was seventy-nine years old. Dot and Kay tried to convince Dot's mother to move into the big house with them, but she preferred to stay in the small house Dot and Kay had built especially for her and Allan.

· · · · · · ·

Dot and Kay filled their off-seasons with the usual pastimes—Dot had convinced Kay to take up bowling, and they were bowling in winter leagues in addition to their work schedules.

Kay kept her job as an auditor for the state tax commission, and Dot barely fulfilled her responsibilities at Hoffman Realty.

Dot also found the time to sit for an interview with *Sports Illustrated* magazine. A three-quarter page picture of her, along with an accompanying story, appeared on page 100 of the magazine. The article headline proclaimed Dot A FEMALE YOGI, as in Yogi Berra, the great Yankees backstop.

"On the field, Catcher Wilkinson is a smart, hard-working ballplayer who doubles as the Rambler manager. Off it, she is a bustling realtor."

At the beginning of 1961, Dot and Kay breathed a sigh of relief as Kay passed the five-year cancer-free milestone.

Unfortunately, the celebration was short-lived. By early spring, they received the news that Kay's cancer had returned in her remaining breast.

"I know at one time we went through the treatment, and they said, 'If you go the five years, you're OK.' Well, she went the five years, but she got it in the other side."

Immediately, Kay underwent a second mastectomy and began an experimental treatment protocol.

"Kay was kind of a special patient at Memorial Hospital. That was the cancer hospital. At one time six doctors had a meeting there and they gave Kay some kind of medication that they had brought in special thinking that it would help her, but it didn't.

"I took care of her most of the time. She still played."

Even with all that was going on in their personal lives, softball remained a driving force for both Dot and Kay. As a result of her receiving All-American honors at shortstop at the world championships in 1960, Kay was eligible to play in the 1961 All-Star series against the three-time World Champion Brakettes, set to take place in mid-July in Connecticut.

"Kay wanted to go with me to the All-Star series in Connecticut. We were going to play two sets of doubleheaders. So we went. Ricki was there too. She was chosen to play second base for the All-Stars. Ricki was always a friend to Kay. They still cared about each other."

To find a spot for Kay on the team, the All-Stars slotted her at third base, a position she'd never played before. Additionally, they made her a coach so that she could feel more a part of the action. On July 13, 1961, Dot and Kay flew from Phoenix to Stratford, Connecticut.

Kay took the field at third base, but it was obvious that she was ailing. She committed two errors in the field and went hitless at the plate for the series. Dot led the All-Stars in hitting, but the Brakettes' stellar pitching staff, featuring Bertha Ragan and twenty-year-old sensation Joan Joyce, shut out the All-Stars over four games and thirty-nine innings of play.

Arizona Republic columnist Arnott Duncan interviewed Dot and Kay together for a feature that ran in the paper on the day they returned from the Connecticut trip.

Of Kay, Duncan wrote:

> *A series of operations this year knocked her out of most active play and left her a coach fearing for a while cancer would seize command. But last week, her doctor told her, "I'm proud of your progress and the possibilities look very good." She has one more surgery scheduled in September "and I hope it's the last."*

"They wouldn't even try it unless they were sure she's recovered and worth it," Miss Wilkinson said. "She's been playing catch and playing pepper and she looks real good now."

At the end of August, Kay flew with the Ramblers to Portland for the 1961 tournament. She was listed as an active player and coach, but she was in no shape to play. Unsurprisingly, Dot's and the team's focus wavered. The Ramblers lost their first two games and flew home.

Kay had her next scheduled surgery after the Ramblers returned from the World Softball Championships.

"The last night before Kay went to the hospital for that September surgery, one of our players, Marge Lange, was there. Kay said, 'I want to drive up to South Mountain. Let's go.' So we went.

"Marge and she and I drove up to South Mountain. South Mountain was kind of a special place to all of us because we spent so much time there. She just wanted to stop and look. . . . That's where she met me.

"We just drove up there and back. It was a terrible road up there, but that's what she wanted to do. The next morning, she went back to the hospital. She knew she was on her last legs I guess, more than we did."

Another surgery in December 1961 followed that September operation. Nothing worked. A feeling of finality settled over Dot and Kay.

In the first months of winter, Kay begged Dot to take her along to the annual softball meeting in California to set the league schedule for the 1962 season. Dot wasn't so sure Kay was up to the trip.

"We had our softball scheduling meeting in California every year to make the schedule for the whole year for all six teams or four teams or however many were in there. Kay wanted to go, and she asked the doctor if she could go. And he said, 'Well, if Dot will make a bed for you in the back of the car, she can take you.' So, that's what I did.

"We stayed at Ricki's apartment. Kay had been sitting in a recliner like the one I have now, and she really liked it. When we got ready to come home, that chair was in the trunk of our car, because Kay and Ricki were good friends. Ricki cared a lot. Kay was very sick, and I know I had to stop on the way home. I didn't know whether I was going to get her home or not, but we made it.

"I'd made a bed for her in the back seat of the car. It was hard for her to go, but she wanted to go, so I took her." It was the last trip Dot and Kay took together.

"As soon as we got home, Kay went to the hospital. She was there for a long time, and I missed a lot of work during that time. I had already almost retired. Ford was still paying me. And I was still doing my part of the escrow department, so I still got money from there. I didn't have very much money.

"The office was still open. Ford had a brother that went in all the time. Ford wasn't doing too good at the time. I tried to stop in at the office every day, even if I just went for a few minutes to try and settle up things and probably to pick up a little money.

"Kay's expenses really piled up. We didn't have any insurance. All the ballplayers Kay had played with from back in Chicago sent donations, and the organizers of the fundraiser had all these names and how much everybody sent. Her friends and fans threw benefits for her to pay her medical costs.

"We had a checking account for that, so I didn't have to pay all those expenses because they were mostly all donated by people. There was money left over, and I still had it on account, so I created the Kay Rohrer Memorial Fund with the excess funds. At one time, while she was in the hospital, Dick Hackenberg, sports editor for the *Chicago Sun-Times*, came and visited her and brought her a check for $1,000 from her fans. She was very popular in Chicago.

"Anyway, that last time she was hospitalized, Kay knew she was dying. Dr. Paul talked to her about it. She asked him if she was dying, and he said 'Yes.' And he asked her, 'Do you and Dot have your things in order?' And she told him we did. Because we'd already made our wills and done everything we were supposed to do.

"I went up there and stayed with her until the very end. The daily nurse was very nice. I was there when Kay's heart stopped. There were nurses all over the place and doctors and all that. They came and they tried to put a needle in Kay's heart and bring her back. That was very sad. The nurse gave me a sedative because she could see how upset I was."

On March 17, 1962, Kay passed away; she was thirty-nine years old.

"Sis King, who was playing for the Ramblers at that time and was staying with me and Kay, went out to Rambler Field and got Daddy Rohrer and brought him in after she died.

"I remember going to Kay's service in the cemetery and my mother and Ruth—we all went together."

"For several years, we gave a Kay Rohrer Award. We bought the trophies and did things. I gave to the hospital a big amount of money at the end for a plaque to put on in Kay's name. It's probably still at Memorial Hospital.

"Kay and I were only together seven years. I'm sure we'd have been together a lot longer if she lived, but she didn't.

"After Kay died, she left all of the investment properties to me, and I was having to pay all that by myself. That wasn't easy because all of that was on payments . . . monthly this and that. And so I had a little tough time making it by myself.

"I didn't realize that I had put that many properties in Kay's name. I knew I had only two or three of them. I didn't realize there were so many more. But they were nothing properties. So there was no money there. In fact, to keep them, I had to pay the payments after she was gone by myself, when we were splitting them before.

"The only money I had was what I was working for. If I sold a house, I got a commission once in a while. I didn't try to sell many houses, but I did have a license. Somewhere along the line, I acquired a license and a notary license and all of that and I got a little money for that. Every new setup that we got in our office when a salesman would sell a house, I'd get so much for that. So I was making a little money on the side, which helped.

"My mother asked Ruth one time—because she knew I was very sad . . . 'Why is Dot so sad?' And Ruth said, 'Oh Mom, she loved Kay so.' Then my mom never asked anymore. That was it."

Dot addressing the crowd on Dot Wilkinson Night at Rambler Field, August 10, 1963. *Courtesy of the Dot Wilkinson Collection*

Dot after
bowling a
740 series.
*Courtesy of the
Dot Wilkinson
Collection*

Part Seven

HEADING
FOR
HOME

20

Turning the Page

OVER THE YEARS, bowling in all those leagues, Dot had become an accomplished bowler. She'd won numerous local events both in singles and doubles.

Shortly before Kay died, she had encouraged Dot to enter the famed Women's International Bowling Congress (WIBC) Championship, the biggest event in all of bowling.

"I wasn't even going to get in it because that was when Kay was sick and I was spending most of my time at the hospital. That year, I only had a 175 average. I always carried a 185 or a 190 average. I just wasn't going into the bowling alley much. I would go only when I had to keep up my league average or whatever I was supposed to do. But I didn't go that often."

That year, the Queens tournament, as it was called, was to be held in Phoenix at the Squaw Peak Lanes, April 23–27, 1962. Dot had submitted her application and the fifty-dollar entrance fee.

As Kay's death neared, Dot wavered about whether to participate in the tournament or withdraw. "Kay is the one that talked me into it, even with how sick she was. She said she wanted me to get in the tournament."

To win, Dot first had to make it to the finals. On April 24–25, she competed in the qualifying rounds. The real test came on Thursday, April 26, when Dot came up against one of the greatest women bowlers in history, Marion Ladewig. The local paper, the *Arizona Republic*, featured a screaming headline:

WILKINSON UPSETS LADEWIG!

Encouraged by an exuberant throng of hometown rooters, Phoenix's amazing Dot Wilkinson pulled a stunning upset by beating famed Marion Ladewig by one pin in a thrilling semifinal match last night in the WIBC Queens Tournament at Squaw Peak Lanes. The score was 752–751.

Tied 570–570 going into the fourth game, Miss Wilkinson picked up the difficult 5–7 split in the fifth frame, and banged two strikes and two spares in the next four to nip Mrs. Ladewig, 182–181.

A thunderous cheer went up from the 800 spectators as Miss Wilkinson picked up the necessary nine pins in the 10th frame. She missed the pin for a spare but didn't need it anyway.

Afterwards, she said, "I was so nervous and glad I didn't really care where the ball went. Even if I had taken my time I don't think I could've made it because I was so jittery."

The dramatic triumph assured Miss Wilkinson at least $1,500 and second place in the nationally publicized event.

She enters the finals at 7 tonight the only undefeated contestant in the original 32-woman field.

Tucson's *Arizona Daily Star* proclaimed, "Phoenician Dot Wilkinson took a heart-stopping victory from former champion Marion Ladewig to reach the finals of the Women's International Bowling Congress Queen's [*sic*] Tournament here last night."

As she later told *Arizona Republic* sports editor Frank Gianelli, "Kay urged me to enter against my protests. I wore her ring the first day and shot an 828 series. I wore it throughout the tournament.

"There were plenty of times when somebody besides me was nudging those pins."

Playing in Kay's memory was not the only motivating factor for Dot.

"My softball fans were there and that's not good for my opponents. A couple of gals that bowled against me from out of town said, 'I'd rather be going up against anybody right now than you.'

"Bowling fans and softball fans are two different people. My ball fans were there rooting for me, and they didn't care what the other person did. If they got a split, that was good for me, bad for them. My fans would hoot and holler. In bowling, you weren't supposed to cheer for someone else's mistake, but my fans did. They didn't know any better."

The finals, televised and broadcast by the CBS network, once again pitted Dot against Marion Ladewig, who now came out of the losers' bracket.

Phoenix's unheralded Dot Wilkinson set the bowling world on its ear last night when she beat Marion Ladewig in a brilliant four game match, 799–794, to capture the WIBC Queens championship.

The pulsating victory brought Miss Wilkinson a $2,000 first place check, a $600 diamond wristwatch, a handsome five-foot trophy and the traditional Queens crown, plus numerous other cash awards.

Her name also flashed across the nation on wire stories since the Queens diadem is considered among the most coveted awards a woman can win in bowling. . . .

Before a packed house of 1,500 in Squaw Peak Lanes, Mrs. Ladewig won the first game by 22 pins, 203–181.

Four straight strikes from the second to fifth frames helped her pile up the points. Miss Wilkinson had two open frames in her opener.

Then Dottie bounced back to pick up six points in the second ten with 211 to her rival's 195. Two splits were costly for Mrs. Ladewig.

The third game proved the most advantageous as she topped Marion, 194–177, to take the lead by 11 pins, 586–575. Mrs. Ladewig only managed one strike. . . .

Mrs. Ladewig, used to pressure after numerous years of participation in national tournaments, put some of it on Dot in the final game. She tied the match in the fourth frame on her second straight strike. The score was 99–77 in the loser's favor. Dot was sitting on a spare.

Up came Dot for her shot. She whipped it in for a strike. She crossed over the other lane and repeated the feat.

Now the pressure was on Mrs. Ladewig again. She got a strike and a spare. It was the sixth frame and the score was 139–135, still Marion's favor.

Dot came back with a strike and a spare. Marion equaled the marks. She still was ahead by four pins and could win the match if Dottie missed.

But Miss Wilkinson didn't. She struck in the 9th and picked up a spare in the 10th for a nice 213 game.

Attention was now on Mrs. Ladewig. If she could strike the last three frames she could win the match and send it into an extra set.

Mrs. Ladewig, considered the greatest woman bowler of all time, rolled the ball carefully. It hit solidly but one pin was left standing.

That was it.

"When I beat Ladewig in the last tournament, when I won the Queens title. . . . If she'd struck out [thrown three consecutive strikes], she would have beaten me. She threw a good ball, but she left one pin standing.

"Why, Sis King flew over the back of the bleachers and onto the lanes because she knew I'd won. Even if Ladewig picked up that pin, she couldn't beat me.

"There was a lot of comment about Sis hugging me right then. Ladewig still had at least one ball left. The WIBC . . . there were a lot of big shots there because they wanted Marion Ladewig to win that tournament. She was one of the best women bowlers around and always had been. She hadn't won the Queens tournament and they wanted her to win. The match was on television, and it was a big thing here in the headlines in the sports pages.

"The WIBC was not happy with me at all. . . . And they didn't like the idea of the local fans who were all rowdy. They're there rooting like softball fans, not like bowling fans. They were there for me. Half the town was there, and the ones that weren't, were watching on television. We'd never had a big thing like that here. That was the biggest tournament they'd ever had.

"That was probably one of the biggest nights of my life. It was funny. I was already being friendly with Ricki then. We'd been writing and talking, and I called her after it was over. There's a newspaper picture of me on the phone with her from the bowling lanes, although they didn't know who I was talking to.

"I told her, 'I just won the Queens.' And she said, 'What's that?' Ricki didn't know what the Queens Tournament was. She had bowled some. She bowled in a league in California. She knew what bowling was, but she didn't know what that tournament was. I said, 'Well, it's big-time so we're going to get to go somewhere.'"

That "somewhere" was the invitation-only Sixth Annual World Match Game Championships to be held at McCormick Place, Chicago, November 15–25, 1962.

"I invited her to go with me to Chicago for a bowling tournament. I asked her if she wanted to go with me—to drive back to Chicago. . . . She said yes."

Dot's surprise victory garnered continued headlines and newspaper columns for days and weeks to come. The *Dayton Daily News* in Ohio proclaimed: DOT WILKINSON SOFTBALLER PIN QUEEN. Similar headlines appeared in such far-flung places as Miami, Fresno, and Cedar Rapids, Iowa.

The *Arizona Sports Journal* took a different angle: Just Pinch Me, Says Dot.

On May 27, in a column in the *Sacramento Bee* called Strikes to Spare, the newspaper tied Dot's Queens success to her softball prowess: International Bowling Queen Champ Is Among Nation's Best in Softball Too.

The day after Dot's big win, Frank Gianelli, in his *Arizona Republic* column, broke another piece of news: Dottie May Reject Check.

> *That $2,000 check Dottie Wilkinson won as Queens bowling tournament champ the other night . . .*
>
> *She isn't going to cash it!*
>
> *"Not until I determine what it will do to my softball amateur status," says the little local dumpling who beat bowling's best in a week of drama at Squaw Peak Lanes.*
>
> *This is Dottie's 30th season as catcher with the Ramblers softball team. "And we're going to try to win the world's championship. We've won it three times previously, got a good club, good spirit. I think we're the best in the country. I want to be with the girls when they prove it," she says simply.*
>
> *There's some long-distance phoning between local softball chiefs and the Amateur Softball Association headquarters back East. Until the issue is determined, Dot's just going to hang onto that check which says she's the best woman bowler in the nation.*

The story was picked up nationally by the Associated Press. In the end, to maintain her amateur status in softball, Dot donated her winnings to the Kay Rohrer Memorial Fund she had established with the leftover monies donated for Kay's medical expenses by her friends and fans.

• • • • • • •

Days after the Queens tournament, Dot traveled to California to see Ricki. On May 5, Ricki put on a memorial game in Orange, California, for Kay. After the game, she presented Dot with a check for $1,132 for the Kay Rohrer Memorial Fund.

"I went over there. I stayed with Ricki and her friend, Cotton [Kay Williamson]. They'd been an item at one time, but now they were just friends. Cotton's brother was living there too. I must have stayed there for a week or something. Ricki was working as a technical illustrator at the Hughes Aircraft plant. The three of them all went to work every morning and I was staying there in the apartment.

"Ricki and I had gotten friendly by that time. After she and Cotton would get in the car, Ricki would come back. I'd hear those heels clacking on the sidewalk coming back to tell me goodbye, and I'm still in bed. So anyway, we got friendly.

"I'd cook for them, and they'd come home, and we'd all have a big dinner every night. When they'd come home from work, I'd have a Swiss steak or something. We had a good time.

"When I got home, Ricki started writing to me and we started writing back and forth."

The softball season progressed, and their long-distance relationship blossomed, with Dot in Phoenix playing for the Ramblers and Ricki in California, playing for the Lionettes.

"Ricki and I were already together. We were still playing against Orange. This one game, she came around third and she said, 'I was not going to try to go home, and he [Bill Allington, the Lionettes' manager] sent me on purpose.'

"So," Dot continued, "I decked her, just like I would any other time. She said, 'I knew I was going to get knocked down.' I probably didn't hit her as hard as I would have a few years earlier.

"When you're playing the ball game, it's a ball game. So, that was it. She was out by a mile. It wasn't even close. She probably tried to knock me down. I probably tried to knock her down. All I remember is, she was out. I probably put the ball on her easy."

When the dust had settled on the season, the Lionettes had won their record sixth world championship, the last Ricki would win with the team before she joined the Ramblers for the 1963 season. The Ramblers finished the 1962 tournament in fifth place, ousted by Portland.

In October, with softball season over, Ricki knew without question that she wanted to spend the rest of her life with Dot. She also understood that Dot never would leave Phoenix. So Ricki gave up everything to be with her. She relinquished controlling interest in the Lionettes franchise, quit her good-paying job at Hughes Aircraft, and forfeited her apartment in Orange. She moved into the house on St. Charles Street with Dot.

In November, they made the trip to the bowling tournament together.

"We were driving to Chicago. We'd been driving all day and reading *Psycho*. That was a big mistake. We stopped every night wherever we happened to be. When we got tired, we'd find a motel. We drove into this place—it backed into apartments—and we'd been reading that dang *Psycho* all day and I couldn't sleep that night. I was scared to death to take a shower. I told Ricki, I said, 'Man, we'd better read something different.'

"That's how we really got started. One of the first things that we did was to drive all day and we'd read to each other. She drove and I drove, and we'd stop at about four o'clock in the afternoon and we'd go to dinner and then come back and watch television or whatever. And so that's how we got to really know each other . . . by driving.

"When you spend that much time just traveling like that, you get to know somebody pretty well. We got along good, and there were no problems."

Dot did not fare well at the tournament, finishing somewhere in the middle of the pack. On the way home, they discussed their future together.

"I remember telling Ricki, 'I have enough to live on. I can make it for ten years.' I had enough properties—an equivalent amount of houses— that I knew I could sell those mortgages and get enough money to get by for a month or whatever if I wanted to. But I hadn't done any of that. I never sold anything that I had. I still had it all. None of them were big properties. They were all little properties, cheap fees, and people were paying me monthly rent on houses I owned and was paying mortgages on. I'm ending up probably putting most of the money they paid me back in the mortgages, but I knew that I could sell them if I had to. And I did have some rentals. I don't know, I was scraping. I thought I was all right."

When they returned home, Ricki searched for positions in her field. Unfortunately, she was unable to find any job in Phoenix that offered the kind of money she was making at Hughes Aircraft.

"When Ricki first came here, she had about $2,500 in cash and so did I. That's what we had. That was our livelihood."

Dot reminded me of a tidbit she'd shared with me early in our friendship, a decade ago, but this time she was ready to tell me the whole story. It was an impressive tale of two women, living life on their own terms at a time when that rarely was done.

"As I told you when I first met you, we looked into buying a flower shop, we looked into any kind of shop to sell clothing or footwear. . . . We were trying to get a business for us, something that we could get into. We looked into many things."

None of them panned out. "And then one day Ricki just said, 'You've got some houses that are in run-down condition. Why don't we fix up one of the houses that you've got and let's do that?' So, we gathered up some stuff. If people threw away lumber, we'd pick it up. That first house we worked on, we had that house for a long time. We'd fix it up and rent it. So that was another $300 bucks a month.

"That was how we got started, and then we just started picking up different places here and there. So, that's when we started with flipping houses before flipping was a popular thing. We worked on those houses, and we used to pick up material for free wherever we could get it.

"To start with, when we'd get one finished, we'd fix it up and we'd rent it. But sometimes, people would come along and buy it while we were working on it. So we did make some sales that way.

"A lot of times, the people we rented to would buy. Later on, when we had more houses, several of them we would rent to, I'd ask them if they were interested in buying them. 'You tell me what you can pay by the month, and we'll work it out.' And that's what we did.

"A lot of the houses brought in about $300 or $350 a month. I didn't have to worry with the business part of it. Ricki did it all. She paid the mortgages and did the banking. Everything that we had was thrown together . . . all of our checkbooks, all of our everything was together. In other words, we threw everything we both had in.

"We had a guy; his name was Lee. He was an old baseball player. He played with Satchel Paige in the Negro leagues. He and his brothers all played baseball way back when. He was a retired plumber. We had a job, and Ford told me his name. We called him, and he came, and he worked for us for several years.

"Finally, he just said, 'Dot, I will teach you how to do this. You don't need to call me and pay me. Just call me and tell me what's wrong, and I'll tell you how to fix it.' He taught me all the plumbing. I learned all that from him. I could use a pipe wrench as good as anybody, and even Ricki did too. Ricki would get down on the floor with a wrench underneath the sinks and stuff.

"We just learned by trial and error. At that time, you didn't have to have a permit to do anything; you could just do it. You made a mistake, too bad.

"We had one house that the front part of it was all finished. It had space in the back with a bunch of rooms and we finished that. It didn't have any electric in it. I wired it all. My nephew, Bob, was an electrician. If we got in trouble, he'd come in and bail us out.

"I learned how to do glass. We bought one house on Pima that was right across from the school, and it had a great big window on the front. The panes were all divided. And I think I put sixty-five or more panes of glass in because the kids had kicked the panes out. They were all broken before we got in. So we learned how to do a lot of glass work.

"We had one place where we bought used plumbing and used stuff. It was a place where they stored the stuff from the houses they were moving to make the freeway. The contractors brought stuff in there. They brought in hot-water tanks and pipes and all kinds of stuff that they were moving from the freeway. The woman who worked there would say, 'Just go through there and pick out whatever you want and then bring it up here.'

She'd charge us fifty-five cents for this, five cents for that. I had to tear the water heaters apart because a lot of the plumbing was together inside and I needed the separate pieces. So I'd sit out in the driveway with my two pipe wrenches and tear them apart. They're like-new galvanized. That was before all this plastic came out. That would have been much easier if we gotten to use those in the first place.

"We always had people that would help us. But we learned. We bought a lot of houses that were really junk. If you bought something for $3,000 and you sold it for $10,000, you thought you were getting rich.

"I took Peanuts one time to show her a house we'd just bought. Oh, and she about died. We had bought three houses on that street . . . on Encinas Lane. They had moved those houses into that neighborhood after the war. They had been lived in, but they were empty. They'd been torn up.

"This one was a big old, three-bedroom thing. It was a junker. I took a picture of it with my Polaroid. I found out the guy who owned it lived in Chicago. I sent him a letter and I said, 'We'll give you $1,000 cash for this house.' He took it.

"So, we fixed that up, and I think we sold it for $10,000 or $12,000. So we did good. But when I took Peanuts there to look at it, it didn't even have any doors. It still had all the windows, but most of the glass was broken out. That's the kind of properties we picked up.

"Ricki and I made a lot of money, but that was because we didn't have to pay for anything. We didn't have to pay commission when we sold a house. We didn't have to go to a title company very often, just once in a while. Whenever we went to a title company, we made the people that bought the house pay for it. I wrote the papers on most of the contracts, because I knew how to do that from Hoffman Realty.

"We used to drive around and look. If we found or saw a house where the windows were broken and the doors were gone and crappy looking, we'd get the address and find out in the tax records who they belonged to. Then we would write them a letter and make them an offer that was ridiculous, and usually they took it. Because nobody wanted to deal with those crappy things.

"At first, we'd find the houses on our own, and then, people started pointing them out to us. We also worked with an investment office. Those girls down there, when they had somebody to foreclose on, they'd tell us about it. So we did that too. They gave us quite a lot of house tips. They'd give us the mortgage or whatever and we'd take it over and go fix it up and then go from there.

"And we managed the houses we had. I did a lot of plumbing. I can remember one New Year's Day. We had a house on 2680 Southgate. A guy called to tell us there was a leak out in the front yard. I went over there and thought I would just go and dig it up and patch it. I ended up putting 130 feet of pipe in on New Year's Day. We used to go and do whatever needed to be done. If somebody called and said that their toilet was stopped or the toilet was leaking, we'd go fix it.

"I've had young girls come up to me in the grocery store and say, 'Hi, Miss Dot. I used to live in one of your houses.' They'd remember me because Ricki and I were good to them. If something was wrong and the client couldn't pay the rent or mortgage, well then, we worked with them. We didn't just kick people out.

"We never went to court with but one person, and that was because he had a shotgun and I was afraid of him. That was the house I mentioned earlier that we bought for $1,000 and we'd fixed it up real good. And it was nice, and we sold it for $10,000 or $12,000.

"We sold it to this guy. He hadn't hardly moved in when we went down there to check because he hadn't done something he was supposed to do. He came out with this gun, so I backed away and got in my car. We just foreclosed on him. I told Ricki, 'We don't need to deal with that.' So we got rid of him.

"One of the biggest jobs that Ricki and I did, maybe the one I'm proudest of, was a big house we had next to the freeway, now on Fourteenth Street. We put sixteen rolls of ninety-pound roofing up on that roof and laid it all. Even though Ricki was afraid of heights, she got up there.

"We were putting rolled roofing on another house down there, and I was over on this end doing one end of it and she was doing the other, and she started sliding down. She said, 'Uh-oh. Here I come. I'm the flying nun.'

"She slid all the way down to the edge. I was ready to go pick her up off the ground, but she stopped right at the bottom of the roof. She was probably scared to death. She was always afraid of heights, and yet she got up there and did it anyway.

"She did a lot of things that she didn't want to do. I would not have what I have today if it wasn't for Ricki. She pushed me into doing more. She would find these houses. She'd see them in the paper and say, 'Come on, we're going to go look at a house.' I would rather have quit.

"I said, 'Haven't we got enough? Haven't we done enough?' She'd say, 'No. Come on, we need to do some more.' I did pretty much what Ricki wanted to do if she asked me to do something.

"When we made any money, we invested it. We didn't spend it. That's not to say we didn't have any fun. We went to Vegas quite regularly for the shows. Ricki and I used to drive up there. We'd get a hotel or a motel. You could go to Vegas, and you could see all these shows. We didn't have to pay anything; we just had to buy three drinks and we could see the shows. We saw Frank Sinatra and Nancy Wilson. . . . We saw a lot of people."

• • • • • • •

When they weren't working or taking trips to Vegas, they were on the bowling lanes or on the softball field. Since winning the Queens tournament, Dot's bowling profile and schedule had picked up steam.

In early May 1963, Dot took time away from the Ramblers' regular season to compete, along with seventeen thousand other entrants, in the Women's International Bowling Congress tournament in Memphis, Tennessee. Many had written her off as a one-hit wonder when she won the Queens—a bowler who hit a hot streak at exactly the right time.

Dot, as always, proved that underestimating her was a mistake. She took the top spot in the prestigious WIBC Singles for a $500 payday. Then she added on a fifth-place finish in the All-Events competition for an additional $200, and managed an eighth-place showing in Division I doubles with her event partner, Dorothy Rowe.

Newspaper columnist Abe Gutierrez took notice:

> *No one can deny now that Dot Wilkinson belongs among the world's best women bowlers.*
>
> *Her outstanding showing in this year's Woman's [sic] International Bowling Congress tournament at Memphis proves that.*

Dot had no time to rest on her laurels, neither to mope when she failed to qualify for the Queens tournament also held in Memphis immediately after the WIBC Championships.

She traveled home to rejoin the Ramblers. Ricki was settling in as the Ramblers' shortstop and comanager of the team, and she'd been busy cooking up a surprise for Dot.

With the assistance of Ramblers publicity director Frank Kuffel, Ricki put together a special Dot Wilkinson Night at Rambler Field. The event took place on Saturday night, August 10, 1963, during a three-game series with Ricki's former team, the Orange Lionettes.

The eight o'clock pregame ceremony was promoted for weeks in the local newspaper, and fans were invited to contribute to a fund for a gift for her. Admission to the game cost $1.50 for box seats and $1 for general admission.

The Boys Club of Phoenix, a sixty-voice choir, sang six songs, including a couple of Dot's favorites. The Maricopa County Sheriff's Office presented a skit titled, "How to Legally Win a Softball Game."

"Ricki just wanted to put that night together. She planned the whole thing. I knew ahead of time that there was going to be an event, because they put a big sign with the date saying AUGUST 10TH WILL BE DOT WILKINSON NIGHT out in front of Rambler Field. But Ricki did a lot of things I didn't even know about in advance for the night.

"It was very thrilling. I remember the wind was terrible that night. We thought it was going to blow us all away.

"God, the presents I got. I got a big gun case that was six feet tall. [Dot and Ricki hunted often, catching doves, ducks, quail, and the like at Lake Pleasant, about twenty miles from their home.] The fans gave me that.

"Louise Curtis, Margie Law, and Amy Peralta all came, and each threw a pitch to me.

"Larry Walker came, which was a big thing. He said I was a good ballplayer and a good athlete. That was kind of a big thing too, coming from him."

In fact, Walker, the old A-1 Queens manager; Joe Hunt of the old Funk Jewels men's team; and Ben Spaulding, who had brought night softball to Phoenix, presented Dot with a huge trophy proclaiming her THE GREATEST ARIZONA ATHLETE OF ALL TIME.

"I know they introduced my mother, and she was standing by the fence. We were out there getting ready to play when the celebration was over, and I had to tell her, 'Mother, you can go sit down now.' Because of course, she couldn't see.

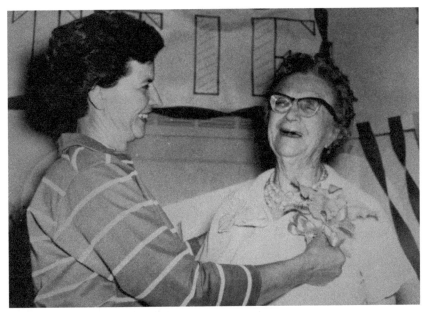

Dot and her mom at the party in the clubhouse on Dot Wilkinson Night at Rambler Field, August 10, 1963. *Courtesy of the Dot Wilkinson Collection*

"I remember going into the clubhouse afterwards, and that's where we had the cake and all of that. That was just for the players and close friends."

The newspaper headline the next day trumpeted: 1,500 PAY DOT WILKINSON TRIBUTE.

> *Miss Wilkinson, who has played in at least 2,400 games and batted for the Ramblers probably 8,000 times, also received telegrams from her legion of friends across the nation. . . .*
>
> *Dottie, who said her biggest previous thrill was the Ramblers' first world title in 1940, told the audience:*
>
> *"There just aren't any words for me to say. I can't say what is in my heart. I've got goose bumps all over."*

The fact that the Ramblers lost the post-celebration game to Orange, 1–0, was incidental.

• • • • • • •

As a consequence of her WIBC Singles win and her Queens title, Dot was selected to represent the United States in the Fifth FIQ (Federation Internationale de Quilleurs, or the International Federation of Bowlers) World Tournament. It was the first time women's bowling would be included in the seventeen-nation tournament. The competition took place from November 3–10, 1963, in Mexico.

"We went to represent the United States, and they paid for everything. Ricki got to go with us, and they paid for her too. I think she paid her flight ticket there. We both went to Chicago because they wanted the entire US team to leave from the same place. So I went from here [Phoenix], which is very stupid. I went from here to Chicago to go back to Mexico. And Ricki, too. We both did. And so, anyway, they paid all of our freight. We had our own room.

"A whole men's team and three other women were chosen to go too. We went to Cuernavaca and Mexico City. When we stayed in Cuernavaca,

Dot in Mexico representing the USA at the FIQ World Tournament, November 3–10, 1963. The federal government paid Ricki's way to accompany Dot on the trip. *Courtesy of the Dot Wilkinson Collection*

one of the men pros told me, 'Dot, you stand right there and throw it right over that line.'

"I never had been a line bowler before [lining up the ball with the arrows on the lane]. I just took the ball and threw it. So, I started doing what he recommended with my first ball, and then my second ball I threw at the pin. After he told me that, I got to where I could hit that same spot all the time and it was working out pretty good. So I did that for a long time.

"I bowled with a gal named Helen Shablis. She was very good. She was number one. She represented the USA in singles, and I was representing the USA with her in the doubles. I saw her several times afterwards at tournaments and still was friendly with her. I got five medals. One was gold and a few were silver and one was bronze."

The *News Leader* of Staunton, Virginia (November 19, 1963), wrote that Dot and Helen Shablis not only won the women's doubles, but they also set a new FIQ tournament record for the United States.

"When everybody else went home from down there, Ricki and I stayed over for a while." Dot figured they deserved the vacation.

• • • • • • •

After her success winning the Queens, the WIBC Singles title, and the medals in Mexico, Dot began to seriously consider a career as a professional bowler. Her first thought was to parlay the wins into a teaching position.

"Naturally, I thought, 'Well, that's going to make a good deal for me. I'll be able to get a job in bowling.' But that was not the way it was. It never turned out. I never got a job in bowling at all. I thought maybe I'd be able to go to work at a bowling lane, but they didn't pay anything. I made more money in real estate. Also, teaching wasn't my thing. So I just really didn't stay with it."

Then Dot pondered life on the professional bowlers' tour. She entered tournaments all over the country.

"I did join professional bowlers and traveled starting in '64 or sometime after. Ricki and I took a trip; I know we went to Salt Lake City and San Francisco and a couple other places. When we came home, I told Ricki, 'I'm not going to do this.' It's too hard, and you'd have to win every tournament. Even then, you'd come out even.

"We were paying our own expenses and paying to get into the tournaments and everything, hoping we were going to win some money. We did win some but not enough."

In fact, in 1964, Dot failed to qualify for the Queens again, she failed to successfully defend her WIBC Singles title that year, and she and Nancy Peterson placed a distant seventh in the national doubles tournament.

"I told Ricki, 'I'm forty-three years old. All these other gals, they bowl fifty lines a day. I don't bowl fifty lines in a week. This is out of my territory.' I didn't like to practice bowling. I just was lucky to be a good bowler because I had control of the ball. I just threw the ball at the pins, and I could hit them."

Still, even having given up on a professional career in the sport, Dot wasn't done bowling. "I still competed in the nationals every year, and I kept bowling in leagues and that type of thing."

And, for the time being, Dot continued to play softball, even though the game was losing its allure with the public. "In the 1940s and '50s,

Ramblers team photo, 1963. Top row, from left to right: Billie Harris, Kay "Cotton" Williamson, Dee Everhart, unknown, Thelma Keith, unknown, Sis King, Theo Wigent, and Jean Lavonovich. Bottom row, from left to right: Dot Wilkinson, Estelle "Ricki" Caito, Roxy Harvey, Bev Soulee, Donna Goehring, unknown. *Courtesy of the Dot Wilkinson Collection*

softball was still fairly new," Dot said. "It was great family entertainment. The ballparks were built in such a way that the fans felt like they were part of the game. They were right there; they could hear everything we said. It was like they were playing."

By the late 1950s and '60s, with the increasing availability of television programming as entertainment; the rise in popularity of other sports such as football, basketball, and tennis; and other things to occupy their time, crowds that had consistently filled Rambler Field and other softball parks around the country had begun to dwindle. As Dot told *Arizona Republic* reporter Dave Hicks in 1963, "We draw hundreds now, where we used to draw thousands."

The heyday of women's softball had passed. Yet, Dot's and Ricki's fire for the game hadn't burned out. As she'd done the previous two years, Dot paid tribute to Kay with a Kay Rohrer Memorial Game.

> Burning candles held by members of her old team, the Phoenix Ramblers, and the visiting Whittier Gold Sox spelled Kay's name across the infield where she scored her biggest triumphs. . . .
>
> While two of Kay's closest friends, Dot Wilkinson and Ricki Caito, struggled with their composure in the background, Theo Wigent spoke for the Ramblers.
>
> "Kay Rohrer is still a member of this team," she said, "although she doesn't trot out to her position any longer. We can never forget her. She gave us inspiration and fight, and left us many fine memories.
>
> "Let no one say that Kay Rohrer finally was put out. Champions always will be on base—and Kay is still with us."
>
> A minute's silence concluded the ceremony for the great infielder who won honors and friends in a career that started with the Chicago Bluebirds and led to the old A-1 Queens of Phoenix and later to seven years with the Ramblers.

Dot, Ricki, and the Ramblers compiled a 35–17 record for the 1964 season and appeared on the field in Orlando, Florida, with a good chance to collect their fourth world championship.

Things took a turn for the worse when an off-the-field incident in the host hotel between the Ramblers and the Utah team cost Phoenix one of their best players.

"Utah was already out of the tournament," Dot remembered, "and we were having a meeting in our room. The door was open because it was hot. The Utah girls made some cracks at us. They were staying down the hall. Dee Everhart, our center fielder and leadoff batter, ran the Utah girls down the hall. One of them ran into the door and hurt her arm.

"The Orange Lionettes' players were staying on the same level as we were. They saw it. After the incident, the Utah gals went back into their room, and I guess their coach, who was a commissioner for Utah, showed up because his player got hurt. He wasn't even there when the incident happened.

"Everybody from Orange stood up for us, but he believed what his team told him, which wasn't the truth of how that girl got hurt.

"The tournament officials—the guy that was running the tournament in Florida and the umpires and the head of the umpires and one other man—held a special meeting the next morning. The Utah coach was at the meeting.

"Those tournament guys believed what the Utah coach said—the made-up story his girls told about what happened. And nobody would believe what I said. I was there for the whole damn thing, and I knew the whole story, and they would not listen to me. So, they threw Dee out of the tournament.

"So we were going to go home, but we put it up for a team vote in our room. Sis King said, 'Well, Dot. We can't quit. We don't want to just give up.' So, we decided to stay.

"For one thing, we had to stay because we didn't have any money. They gave you so much for mileage, and we hadn't gotten ours. And if we'd gone home, we wouldn't have had enough money to even get gas to go home because none of us had any money then. So, it was a bad situation. We stayed and played. Then we got rinky-dinked by the umpires twice more."

As Henry Landress of the *Orlando Evening Star* described it:

> *The Orlando Rebels roared into the finals of the winners division of the Women's World Softball Tournament with an unusual 1–0 win over Phoenix, Arizona, that caused tempers to flair [sic]. . . .*
>
> *The play was protested vigorously by manager Dot Wilkinson— but to no avail.*

"The first loss we had was the one where they called that our third baseman, Roxy Harvey, blocked the runner. There was a first-and-third play, and Ricki was backing up the play. She had the ball in her hand behind third base, and they gave the runner home plate and that was the winning run.

"It was a sliding play where they both slid into third base. There was no force. We missed the play. The ball bounced off the runner's body, and Ricki was backing it up, so she was right there. There was no way that runner could have gone home without a play. She might've been safe, I don't know about that, but Ricki was standing there holding the ball. Even the umpires, after the game was over, they admitted they'd made a bad call when they called interference and gave that girl home plate. So that was the winning run.

"Then we played Orange the next day. Orange put on a squeeze play, and I had the plate blocked out. Sharon Bacus, the Orange runner, tried to score on Nancy Ito's bunt. Man, she never even touched home plate yet, and they call her safe. Everybody on Orange knew she was out. That was the winning run.

"That cost us that game and knocked us out of the tournament. So we got two bad calls in different games. We had a good team in Florida and we had a good draw and we were in a good position and everything was working fine, and then Dee got disqualified and we got the bad calls."

For Dot and Ricki, that was the last straw. "On our way home that year, Ricki and I were driving to the ballpark, and we said, 'We're not going to go through this anymore. No more national tournaments to get your heart broken. You work so damn hard physically to get your team there, and then you get screwed.'"

· · · · · · ·

But Dot and Ricki didn't quit right away. They led the Ramblers to yet another state championship and one last world championships appearance, the team's twenty-eighth in their thirty-three-year existence.

Much to Dot's and Ricki's chagrin, after defeating the defending champion Lionettes, 1–0 in the first round, the Ramblers dropped the next two games, finishing a disappointing fourteenth in the standings.

On Monday of Labor Day weekend 1965, the Ramblers played their last game, fittingly, at Rambler Field, against the Huntington Park Blues.

"Ricki and I just decided, that's it. A lot of the younger players weren't happy because a lot of them wanted to play, and that's why I encouraged them to go to Sun City.

"Half of the team wanted to keep playing and became the Sun City Saints. They played in the ASA. They went into the Pacific Coast League and played against Orange. But the league had dwindled down to where there weren't as many teams then. The whole system was starting to peter out.

"I gave the Saints our batting machine, balls, bats, and all the equipment. I said, 'I'll give you everything but our name. You can't take the Ramblers. The Ramblers are going to retire.' I didn't have anything to do with Sun City. Ricki and I got out of it completely.

"When we made up our minds that we were retiring, we just retired the whole thing. We retired the Ramblers. We tore down the ballpark because we owned everything on the land, but we did not own the ballpark. We sold the seats for a dollar and a quarter apiece. Some club bought a lot of it. Ford got half of the profits and I got half because we were the only ones that put any money into it.

"Actually, when I said we tore the ballpark down physically, we did. Our club room that we had at Rambler Field, we had everything in there. It was all redwood siding and all that.

"Ricki and I hauled all that lumber to St. Charles in my truck and a trailer. We had a second lot in the back of St. Charles, and we built a big room out in the back of our place on St. Charles.

"We just stacked all that lumber out there to start with, and then Joe, my brother-in-law, who had built my mother's house, told us how, and so we built a twenty-four-foot-by-twenty-four-foot room out there.

"We still were flipping houses. That was another reason we were glad to retire—because we were working pretty hard. We weren't getting paid, and we were working on our own and doing all the work. It wasn't easy. So we figured it was time for us to quit.

"After we retired the team, Ricki and I were playing golf and racquet-ball and that kind of stuff. I said to Ricki, 'Are you missing playing?' She said no, and I wasn't either. We'd had it, I guess."

And so, the much-feared and revered PBSW Ramblers closed up shop, after a thirty-three-year run. Dot, a three-time world champion and record-setting nineteen-time All-American, was on board for every bit of it.

A small item appeared in the *Arizona Republic* on December 11, 1965. The headline read: RAMBLERS SAY ADIOS TO SOFTBALL. The story was written by longtime sports editor Frank Gianelli:

> *RAMBLERS, P.B.S.W., 33, passed away Thursday of natural causes. Survived by hundreds of daughters and a few friends. Internment already completed at Rambler Field. R.I.P.*
>
> *The strong heart of the Phoenix Ramblers softball team gave up yesterday—long after the basic body had become a corpse.*
>
> *Team manager and captain Dottie Wilkinson, whose 33-year playing career matched that of the club, announced:*
>
> *"We won't field a team next year."*
>
> *Financial trouble, lack of public interest, scarcity of competent girl athletes forced reluctant admittance the Ramblers had outlived an era.*
>
> *In a society of changing moods, often there is no room for what has gone before. The Ramblers were so caught in a world where the sports pace had quickened, but there was insufficient market for their softball talent.*
>
> *In their heyday, the Ramblers played to crowds of 8,000 to 10,000, won the world championship in 1940, 1948, and 1949, and were runners-up eight times.*

They went to 28 world tournaments. They won the Pacific Coast title five times. They placed eight women in softball's National Hall of Fame.*

Their rivalry with the A-1 Queens gave Phoenix some of its most eventful action in the late '40s and early '50s and they brought in the best offer.

Miss Wilkinson, a team member since she was 9,† won 19 All-America selections. Originally a second baseman, she turned to catching and played that position 27 years.

"It was time to quit," she said yesterday. "I'd rather have fans remember me as I was, than watch me decline and say, 'I knew her when she was good.'"

---

* The author was unable to verify the number of Pacific Coast titles won by the Ramblers. In addition, the Ramblers placed seven, not eight players in the National Softball Hall of Fame.

† She was actually eleven.

Dot and me sharing a laugh while signing autographs following the
live taping of my documentary about Dot. Filmed September 20, 2014.

Photo: Laine Causey, Courtesy of Lynn Ames

Part Eight

EXTRA
INNINGS

21

Basking in the Afterglow

IN JANUARY 1970, five years after she'd hung up her spikes, Dot was elected to the National Softball Hall of Fame. The induction ceremony wasn't held at the museum in Oklahoma City. Instead, one of Dot's fiercest opponents, the Orange Lionettes, hosted a Hall of Fame extravaganza for her in July, between games in the annual National All-Star series.

Ricki was there, of course, as was Billie Harris. Many former Lionettes poured onto the field from the stands to wish Dot well, and congratulatory telegrams came in from the Fresno Rockets and former players. An official from the ASA presented Dot with her Hall of Fame plaque.

Dot stepped up to the microphone and quipped, "Boy, it's really a nice change of pace to be getting applause here in Orange instead of boos."

The crowd gave her a standing ovation.

Three years later, Ricki received her Hall of Fame plaque in Sun City.

And the accolades kept coming. In 1974, Dot was inducted into the Arizona Softball Hall of Fame. In 1979, the honor came from the Phoenix Women's Bowling Association Hall of Fame. That was followed two years later by the Arizona Women's Bowling Association Hall of Fame.

But two hall of fame ceremonies in particular stand out for Dot.

The first took place in 1976, when she was tapped for the Arizona Sports Hall of Fame (then known as the Phoenix Press Box Hall of Fame). Previously, Dot had been honored by that organization with an achievement award. The letter asking her to accept that first award was dated January 9, 1963, and read as follows:

> *Dear Miss Wilkinson:*
>
> *It is my pleasure to inform you that you have been selected to receive a Phoenix Press Box Association Athletic Achievement award.*
>
> *The award will be presented at the annual P.P.B.A. Sports Award Dinner on February 5, at the Westward Ho.*
>
> *As this is somewhat of a "male only" function, except for special awards, the P.P.B.A. would like to invite you to dinner at the Kiva Club in the Westward Ho on that evening. Then after dinner you will be escorted to the Thunderbird Room to receive your award. Dinner will be served at 8 PM. . . .*
>
> *Sincerely,*
>
> *Len Johnson*
>
> *Special Award Chairman*
>
> *Phoenix Press Box Association*

"There were a bunch of times they'd tell me they were going to award me with something or other and I'd go. But you could never go where the men were. I'd have dinner upstairs with some of the wives or something. And, then when they wanted to give the award, I would go down there to get it."

So, in 1976, when the Press Box Hall of Fame reached out to Dot again, this time to make her the first-ever female inductee, she spelled out the conditions under which she would be willing to accept the award.

"When I was put into the Arizona Press Box Hall of Fame in 1976, no women ever were allowed. They were going to give me this award, and

I said, 'Well, I'm not going to go. If my sister can't come and my mother can't come, and my teammates and my friends can't come, then I'm not going.' So they changed the rules.

"So we went. And, when I got up to give my speech afterwards, why, I got a few boos from some of the men in the audience. I laughed and I said, 'Thank you. Now I feel at home. I get booed half the time when I'm playing ball, so now I feel at home.'

"Then, they gave me a standing ovation. It was nice, though. This one man said, 'Well, my wife's been bugging me for years to get to go to this. And she could never go.' From then on, the women were always welcomed. Sometimes we just have to stand up."

The second hall of fame event that Dot holds close to her heart occurred in 1990. Finally, after much cajoling from the Phoenix Women's Bowling Association, Dot received a letter informing her that she'd been selected for induction into the National Bowling Hall of Fame.

"The Phoenix Association had been trying to get me in for a long time. The induction ceremony was going to be in Florida. So, Ricki and I went to Tampa for a week. We had a ball. We had parties with the bowlers, but we also went out with some friends who came in from Stuart, Florida, for the ceremony. They took us a lot of places down there. So we had a real good time.

"There were over three thousand women bowlers at the induction ceremony; it was part of their annual meeting. I was very impressed with Marion Ladewig [the champion bowler Dot had upset in her first Queens tournament final]. I know she was not happy with me, but she was a good sport. She walked with me from the very top of that auditorium all the way down to the stage, which I thought was very classy.

"Ricki got a front row seat. She was sitting right down there yipping at me when I went by. And Dorothy Rowe, who was the president of the Phoenix Association, was on the microphone.

"I gave a pretty good speech there. I thanked everybody. I thanked them for the honor, and I thanked all the people I bowled against and I told them that I appreciated it."

Dot being inducted into the National Bowling Hall of Fame, 1990.
Courtesy of the Dot Wilkinson Collection

22

Adjusting to Life
After Softball

WHEN DOT WASN'T BUSY RECEIVING HONORS, she and Ricki were settling into a new, slightly different post-softball life.

"Our real estate business wasn't just a five-days-a-week job. We
worked all seven. I went out many Sundays and worked and so did Ricki.
We tried not to do any planned work on Saturday or Sunday, but if anything came up, then that's where we'd be.

"For fun, we were playing golf on Sundays with a group. We had about
sixteen girls that would come out every Sunday and we just played. After
we got through playing . . . they had a place where you could get beer and
pizza. So we'd all end up over there. So that was a fun time."

Dot and Ricki also became more friendly with some of their old softball foes. Kay Rich and Bernie Amaral of the Fresno Rockets, Jo McLachlan of the Lionettes, and Dot's old friend and teammate, Jessie Glasscock,
had motor homes up in northern California. Dot and Ricki visited them,
a trip that became an annual ritual, along with reunions of softball players
that took place around the Dinah Shore Open in Palm Springs, California.

"We always looked forward to those trips."

But what really made Dot's face light up was an unexpected purchase she and Ricki made in the early 1970s.

"We bought a cabin in Williams, Arizona, from friends. The cabin was a five-hour drive from Phoenix. We had known Helene and Gee for quite a long time.

"We went on a vacation up to Greer. A whole group of us went fishing. Helene and Gee were telling us about this cabin they had, and they said they were getting ready to get rid of it. So they asked Ricki and me if we wanted it.

"I said, 'Oh hell, we can't afford it. We're paying on St. Charles now. We can't pay on another. We're paying nineteen dollars a month, and that's about all we can do.' They said, 'Well, come on up and look at it and we'll spend some time.'

"So, we went up and spent some time with them. We loved it, and when we got ready to come home, on the way out, Helene said, 'Dot, if you want this cabin, you can have it for $6,000. However you want to pay for it all over time is OK.'

Dot and Ricki at their cabin in the early 1970s. *Courtesy of the Dot Wilkinson Collection*

"So, we wrote a contract and we paid them $6,000—$50 a month, 6 percent interest. And even when Ricki and I got any money, we didn't pay it off. We just paid it off fifty dollars a month.

"We just made it through the whole contract. Best buy we ever made. Right now, that place is probably worth $150,000 or something like that.

"Instead of going away lots of places, we went to the cabin at least one week out of every month. We used to have a lot of parties up at the cabin.

"I can remember one weekend up there we had twenty-six people. We could sleep six adults, and then we had a couch in the living room that converted into a bed. But that was hard because the living room wasn't that wide, so it was hard to flip a bed out. So sometimes I'd sleep on the couch, but most of the people came in motor homes and they'd bring their dogs.

"We had more dogs than people up there. Ricki and I always had dogs, and everybody else brought their dogs too. We had a horseshoe pit out in the back, and we had contests all the time, doubles matches. There's only so much you can do when you're out at the cabin. So that's what we did—and barbecued and ate and had fun."

• • • • • • •

Although Dot was enjoying life after softball, important losses continued to weigh heavily on her heart. On January 8, 1973, after a six-month steady decline, Dot's mother passed away. Ricki and Dot had moved her into the main house on St. Charles as she lost strength and mobility.

"She just got weaker, and she got to where I was the only one that could lift her up and down. I had to tell her that I was going to take her to the hospital. I rode with her in the ambulance, and on the way there she said, 'You're taking me to the hospital to die, aren't you?' Mom was ninety-one years old and had never even been in the hospital. She'd had four children, all of them born at home.

"I said, 'No, Mom I'm trying to make it easier for you because you're uncomfortable.'

"And she said, 'That's OK.' She was all right with going to the hospital and dying. She only lasted about fifteen days."

Dot, her sister Ruth, and her brother Bill held services for their mom two days later. Their older sister, Joan, had passed away twenty years earlier.

At fifty-one years old, Dot, who had never lived without her mother, was bereft.

Ricki, on the other hand, was anxious to move forward. "Ricki wanted a house of our own, so she kept looking in the paper. It was really hard for me to move from St. Charles, because I knew I was leaving my sister, who still lived two doors down from us. Also, we had done a lot of work on that house. We put the block fence around the front because we had the dogs. Kay and I put a pool in there. Ricki and I did a lot more after that.

"We looked at a lot of houses before we finally decided on this one [Dot referred to the sunroom where she was telling me this story] and bought it in 1974. The boys that lived here had a 6 percent interest deal. We bought them out.

"They had just put in this pool; it was brand-new. It didn't have anything around the outside of it. It had a deck and a fence, and that was it. And when Ricki and I came to see this house, the guy said, 'Come on, I'll show you the outside.'

"I walked out there to the pool, and there was his girlfriend out there, and she was naked as a jaybird. I turned around and went back inside. I don't know what Ricki did. We laughed about that for a long time.

"When Ricki and I bought this house, we both had twenty-year insurance policies. She cashed in one of her insurance policies, and I did too. They were the kind that were all paid up and we could never earn more on them than what they were worth right then.

"We used them to buy this house, to get the equity to make the down payment. We had a mortgage. We paid on it and doubled up on the payments and tried to pay it off. Took a while. But I really liked this house, so it made it easier."

· · · · · · ·

In 1976, the softball world reached out to Dot and Ricki once more. A new, ambitious, ten-team professional women's softball league was starting up. The International Women's Professional Softball Association was cofounded by tennis great Billie Jean King and Dennis Murphy, the founder of the World Hockey Association, and backed by stalwart stars such as pro golfer Jane Blalock and softball royalty Joan Joyce.

"Arizona got a pro team called the PhoenixBirds. Some guy owned the franchise. He didn't have the money to finish it. The team moved to Prescott, and they asked Ricki and I if we'd coach them up there.

"So, we went to Prescott and coached and stayed in a motel for the two weeks they were there. We beat Connecticut [formerly the Brakettes] one game. Then, the team folded up because of the money. They weren't making it.

"Ricki and I tried to keep the team together. With a few others, we were going to try to move the team to Phoenix and have them play out of here and get back into that league. There were four or five of us here that put up some money to do it, and we paid the players' salaries the first couple of pay cycles.

"The other people all got out of it. So it cost Ricki and I a little money—about $1,000 in the end—because we ended up on the tail end of it for payroll taxes. We really had good intentions of bringing the team to Phoenix. But it just never worked out."

· · · · · · ·

Having set softball aside for the last time, Dot and Ricki spent what leisure time they had at the cabin, traveling to California to see friends and focusing on their other sporting endeavors.

Ricki developed diabetes and neuropathy in her feet. The former, she and Dot controlled with diet. The neuropathy made playing sports problematic.

"Ricki and I kept bowling in leagues all the time. We went to the national tournaments every year. Ricki usually went with somebody else, and I went with a higher-average team. The last year we went to the national tournament that Ricki was able to go, we went on the same team, and she fell on the approach to a throw.

"When that happened, she got disqualified and we had to bowl with four bowlers the rest of the time. So that was tough. I can't remember where that was, but we were bowling with Betty George and Helen Cunningham and Sharon Coles. They were very gracious about it. They understood.

"We had a pretty good team. We thought we had pretty good chances. Not after that. What happened was, Ricki stuck on the lane. Well, I went flying out, because she fell clear over and went over the lanes and down in the gutter.

"So, I went running over there and hell, I stepped in the lane and my feet went out from underneath me. So, I had to change my shoes and do everything before we could ever get going. That was a bad tournament. Ricki was embarrassed, and so was I. But we went ahead and bowled. We didn't do too bad, the four of us.

"That was the end of that level of bowling competition for us, although we kept playing locally after that."

In fact, Dot continued to enter some senior tournaments for many years to come, only hanging up her bowling shoes when she was eighty-five years old. "At that point, I had to tape up my ankle. I had to wrap up my finger to where I could just lift enough. I just put the ball down there. I could still hit the spot, but I didn't have much on the ball."

Golf remained another passion. "Ricki and I used to go play golf every day. We always walked the course all the way around and pulled our own wagon. Ricki would say, 'I got to stop for a while.' And I wondered why. But I never really knew.

"We played a lot of golf, and then the golf pro told us we'd have to ride in a cart. We didn't want to do that. Ricki and I talked about it and Ricki said, 'The only reason we're doing this is to get the exercise, and if we have to ride in a cart and get out and hit the ball and then get back in the cart, we quit.'

"Not only that, but Ricki's hands got bad, and she couldn't play golf anymore. She must have had some kind of arthritis or something in her whole body.

"So we started playing racquetball. There's a court about a few blocks from here. We went there every day and spent about thirty minutes and just hit the ball back and forth and got more exercise than we got all day out there playing golf."

. . . .

Time and overuse were taking a toll on Dot's and Ricki's bodies. In 1985, when Dot was sixty-four and Ricki was sixty-one, they gave up actively flipping houses . . . almost.

"In 1990, I think it was, Ricki saw an ad in the paper for a house for sale. We took Peanuts with us. The house had a mortgage of a couple thousand dollars. We offered $20,000 cash for the house and said we'd assume the existing mortgage.

"The first renters we had were a good couple. They rented the place for $650 a month. The next renters were an older couple. They had a fire that burnt the place down. We rebuilt it. It was a three-bedroom house with an enclosed, converted carport.

"Ricki and I started getting calls from the people next door to the place. They said there were strange things going on over there—cars coming and going at all hours. Turns out, the renters were subletting the carport to a prostitute who was doing business out of the driveway, and there were drug problems and all kinds of nonsense. The police came and made all kinds of arrests.

"We sold the house for cash to a guy we'd made a bunch of previous deals with. And I said to Ricki, 'That's it. No more houses.' So, that was our last flipped house. By that time, between the houses and our investments, we had more than a million dollars.

"Since then, we've sat back and just kept collecting income on the houses we already owned. We were still doing that right up until the day Ricki died."

. . . .

Dot got wistful as she looked back at her life. "It wasn't always easy. Not even for Ricki and me. We went through some rough patches. Ricki struggled with depression. At one point, it got so bad she checked herself into the Wickenburg psychiatric facility [50 miles northwest of Phoenix]. I visited her once a week, every week, for the three weeks she was there. Her doctor finally diagnosed her depression and put her on medication. Things got a lot better after that."

The losses piled up. Dot's brother-in-law, Joe, and Ruth and Joe's youngest son, Jo-Jo, passed in 1985, Joe from natural causes, and Jo-Jo from a gunshot wound he suffered as a bystander in a gas station robbery.

Ford Hoffman died in 1989. Although he and Dot had long ago reconciled, Dot was unable to attend his funeral because she was away at a bowling tournament at the time.

Dot's beloved sister, Ruth, whom she continued to see every day, even after Dot and Ricki moved from the St. Charles house, succumbed to a stroke in 1990.

Cancer claimed Peanuts in 1999.

In 2000, Dot's brother, Bill, passed away, leaving Dot the only remaining Wilkinson of her generation.

Dobbie, who suffered from dementia late in life, continued to call Dot her closest friend. They remained in close contact. Dot visited Dobbie on her deathbed. Dobbie passed away November 16, 2018, at the age of ninety-five.

23

Promises Kept

IN 1999, THE STATE OF ARIZONA named Dot the eighth-best Arizona athlete of all time. The *Arizona Republic* gave Dot a higher ranking, naming her Arizona's sixth-best athlete of the twentieth century. Dot was the only woman to make the top ten on either list.

Although it's been a long time since she ruled the local and national headlines for softball and bowling and she's no longer a household name in the region, Dot has not been forgotten.

One day in May 2016, she called me and asked me to bring over my softball glove.

"Why?"

"I need to have a game of catch with you."

My eyebrows rose up into my hairline. "Why?"

"Because the Arizona Diamondbacks asked me and Billie to throw out the first pitch at their game tomorrow night. I want to make damn sure I don't bounce the thing in front of home plate."

I laughed but dutifully showed up with my glove and a nicely broken-in softball. There, on the street in front of Dot and Ricki's house, then ninety-four-year-old Dot and I played a ten-minute game of catch. She never bounced the ball once.

The next night, I accompanied Dot and Billie onto the field, stepping back as they crossed the foul line to a thunderous, well-earned ovation from the crowd of thirty thousand on hand to see the Diamondbacks play at Chase Field. Dot waved to the crowd, stepped up in front of the mound, and threw a strike to the catcher behind home plate. She was having the time of her life.

As Dot and I sat and chatted over one of our leisurely lunches a few days after the event, she paused with her miniature hamburger halfway to her mouth. "Do you think Ricki's waiting for me up there?"

"I know she is."

On May 13, 2016, Dot Wilkinson and Billie Harris threw out the first ball at Major League Baseball's Arizona Diamondbacks game in Phoenix. Dot and Billie have been close friends since 1950, when Billie first joined the Ramblers. *Courtesy of Sarah Sachs/Arizona Diamondbacks*

"You know, all my friends are up there. All my teammates and the opponents who became my friends. I don't even know if I could make the team if they have a softball team up there."

I smiled ruefully. "Trust me, Dot. You'll make the team."

"You know, I talk to Ricki all the time. Every night before bed. Crazy, huh?"

I assured her it was not the least bit crazy.

"Sometimes, I go out to the cemetery, and I talk to Ricki a little longer out there. When I'm puzzled about something, I ask her, 'What I should do?' And then I say, 'I wish you were here to answer my questions.' But she's not.

"I carry her picture in my wallet. After she died, I was going through her drawers, and I found some love poems she'd written. Those are in my wallet too. She never gave them to me.

"I never knew she felt the way she talks about in the poems. I wish I had.

"Maybe I'll get to see her again and tell her how I felt. I should've done a better job of that."

I assured Dot that Ricki knew exactly how much she loved her, and that Ricki felt the same way. I feel absolutely certain in this conviction. After all, Ricki told me as much, that last time I saw her, when she asked me without words to pitch relief—to take the ball and take care of her Dot.

· · · · · · ·

In 2016, the Arizona Softball Hall of Fame honored Dot with its very first Lifetime Achievement Award. They asked me if I'd give the speech presenting Dot with the award. It was one of the greatest honors of my life.

Dot was unaware in advance that I was the one who would speak and present her with the plaque. What she was aware of was that I was bringing someone very special with me that night.

"There's someone I want you to meet."

"Oh?"

"Yes. It's important to me, Dot."

"Well, if it's important to you, it's important to me."

"I want you to chaperone our first date."

"Oh," Dot said, drawing out the word. "You'd trust me to do that?"

"No. But I'm going to do it anyway."

When we arrived at Dot's to pick her up and take her to the awards banquet, I made the introduction.

"Dot, this is Cheryl. Cheryl, this is my dear friend Dot."

I could see the gleam in Dot's eyes as she took Cheryl's measure. I watched as she put Cheryl through her paces. And I smiled at the joy that lit up Dot's face when she pulled me aside a little later.

"I think I'm in love with her," Dot said.

"Oh, no you don't," I answered. "This one's mine."

When the time came, it was Dot who stood up for Cheryl and me at our wedding.

· · · · · · ·

The banquet hall at the Arizona Softball Hall of Fame event was full as I looked out over the crowd. I didn't need any notes. I said what was in my heart. Dot was the greatest catcher ever to play the game of women's softball. She would say the game gave her everything, and she gave everything to the game. I'm not sure who was luckier.

As I finished, the crowd rose to its feet to give Dot one last, long, standing ovation. I smiled as I thought about Ricki and all of Dot's friends and teammates applauding her from heaven. Yes, there most certainly will be a place for Dot Wilkinson on that all-star team in heaven, and what a team for the ages it will be.

Epilogue

ON MONDAY, MARCH 13, 2023, I received a text letting me know that Dot was unresponsive. She'd been admitted to the hospital for the very first time in her life the previous week. After three days, she'd been released to return home on hospice care.

I flew to Phoenix immediately to be with her.

I'll always hold close the look of pure joy on Dot's face as recognition dawned when I came into view.

She exclaimed, "You came!" She reached out for a hug and kiss.

We had a joyous golden hour in which we both said everything we needed to say. Then she slipped into sleep. She rallied again briefly for half an hour the next day.

Dot passed away several days later, at 3:30 AM, Saturday, March 18, 2023. She was 101.

There will never be another like the indomitable Dot Wilkinson—trailblazer, pioneer, all-time great. Before there was Billie Jean King, before there was Title IX, before the United States women's soccer team fought for pay equity, there was Dot, living life on her own terms and making it possible for all the women and young girls behind her to do the same. That will be her greatest legacy.

Acknowledgments

A BIOGRAPHY LIKE THIS DOESN'T HAPPEN IN A VACUUM. First and foremost, my deepest gratitude to indomitable Dot, for her graciousness, her openness, and her willingness to share with the world so much of herself and her story.

To Ricki, for entrusting me with Dot's extra innings.

To Ford Hoffman, a man way ahead of his time, for being a guiding star and beacon of light and for recognizing Dot's potential, harnessing her talent, and fighting for Dot's right and the rights of all female athletes to be seen, heard, and taken seriously.

To the members of the PBSW Ramblers, for your zest, power, and excellence on the field and your grace off the field.

To Carol Spanks, Kay Rich (deceased), Sis King (deceased), Virginia "Dobbie" Dobson Bickle (deceased), Shirley Judd Wade (deceased), Rose Mofford (deceased), Jo McLachlan, Nelda Majors, Billie Harris, and Bonnie Bryant, for regaling me with stories that brought the "old days" back to life. The book is so much richer because of all of you.

To Stormy Irwin and Mary Littlewood, for your dedication to chronicling the game.

To Karen Hill for sharing your notes and your graciousness.

To Cathi Jones; to the Chicago Public Library Special Collections Department; to Alexis Burson, humanities and social sciences librarian, DePaul University; and the Chicago Collections member institutions, for helping me chase down rabbit holes.

To Renee James, Curator of the Greater Arizona Collection at the Arizona State University Library and Archives, who scoured through boxes of old photographs to find me needles in haystacks.

To my literary agent, Stacey Glick, for championing me and Dot; my editor at Chicago Review Press, Jerome Pohlen, for recognizing the importance of Dot's story and helping me tell this story to the world; and Ben Krapohl and Cathy Jones, for their excellent guidance and attention to detail.

Finally, and most especially, to my amazing wife, Cheryl, for taking this journey with me, for giving me the support and space to do the work, for spending countless hours scanning, documenting, and organizing photographs, documents, and memorabilia, and for loving Dot as much as I do.

Notes

2. Dot and *Eyes on the Stars*
 "The PBSW Ramblers, Arizona girls": *Arizona Republic*, September 20, 1938.

11. The High School Years
 "We pass them up": Jerry McLain, "Arizona's Larruping Lassies," *Arizona Highways*, August 1949, 27.
 "We still have a bad taste": *Arizona Republic*, September 15, 1937, Section Two, page 3.
 "He said, 'You're the catcher'": "Arizona Athletes of the Century," *Arizona Republic*, Saturday, December 18, 1999.
 "We went to the show": Margaret Vance's Daily Log Courtesy of the Arizona Historical Foundation, University Libraries, Arizona State University, as quoted in Mary L. Littlewood, *The Path to the Gold* (Columbia, MO: The National Fastpitch Coaches Association, 1998), 17.

13. The 1940 World Softball Championships
 "If the PBSW Ramblers of Phoenix": "PBSW Girls Gain Meet Semifinals," *Arizona Republic*, September 8, 1940.

14. The War Years
 "One summer evening in 1934": Raymond F. Law, "National Girls Softball Champs Stress Youth, Versatility, Fight," *Associated Press*, as it appeared in the *Tucson Daily Citizen*, August 13, 1941.
 "Winner up to yesterday": "World Champs Get Ready," *Arizona Republic*, Sunday Morning, July 27, 1941.
 "Miss Wilkinson is rated one": "Ramblers After Softball Crown," *Arizona Republic*, August 16, 1942.
 "All-American catcher": "Ramblers After Softball Crown."
 "The particular type of employees": "AiResearch Ready to Start Hiring," *Arizona Republic*, October 17, 1942.
 "Dot wasn't a poor sport": "Wilkinson Wasn't Good at Losing," *Arizona Republic*, Saturday, December 18, 1999.
 "I remember one Queens-Rambler game": "Ex-Queen Lois Recalls Duels," *Arizona Republic*, Thursday, June 25, 1959.
 "It was the 14th inning": Clipper Williams, "Girls Play Game 'For Keeps,'" *Arizona Republic*, Arizona Magazine, December 9, 1945.

15. Keeping Her Eye on the Ball

"was constructed with softball in mind": Jerry McLain, "Arizona's Larruping Lassies," *Arizona Highways*, August 1949, 39.

"Phoenix Ramblers declared ineligible": "Queens, Ramblers Both Held Ineligible," *Arizona Republic*, September 5, 1946.

"Report Phoenix Queens have overtraveled": "Queens, Ramblers Both Held Ineligible."

"So, the Queens and Ramblers spent": "Queens, Ramblers Both Held Ineligible."

"Please be informed that effective": *Arizona Republic*, January 16, 1947.

"home plate, the catcher and umpire": Arnott Duncan, "Wilkinson, Rohrer All Stars," *Arizona Republic*, Sunday, July 16, 1961.

"Ramblers are world champs": Jerry McLain, "Arizona's Larruping Lassies," *Arizona Highways*, August 1949, 38.

16. We Are the Champions

"The game of softball is": McLain, "Arizona's Larruping Lassies."

City Softball Truce Is Told: "City Softball Truce Is Told," *Arizona Republic*, February 29, 1948.

"I was 16 or 17, and": Arnott Duncan, "Wilkinson, Rohrer All Stars," *Arizona Republic*, Sunday, July 16, 1961.

"The big game of the week": "Queen Nine, Ramblers to Renew Rivalry," *Arizona Republic*, May 27, 1948.

"The Ramblers, defending champions": "Rambler, Monrovia Nines Open Double-Card Tonight," *Arizona Republic*, May 29, 1948.

"An all-time All-America girls' softball": Arnott Duncan, "All-Time All America Softball Girls Team Selected by Pilots," *Arizona Republic*, September 28, 1948.

"The parade will end at": "Champion Ramblers to Be Feted Tonight," *Arizona Republic*, October 1, 1948.

"Mention the Ramblers": Jerry McLain, "Arizona's Larruping Lassies," *Arizona Highways*, August 1949, 36.

"At Portland, the Dieselettes finished": *ASA Balls and Strikes*, interview with Marie Wadlow, March 1957, as quoted in Mary L. Littlewood, *The Path to the Gold* (Columbia, MO: National Fastpitch Coaches Association, 1998), 40.

18. The Winds of Change Are Blowing

"I'd never seen women play": Stormy Irwin, newsletter, 1963. Parentheticals are bracketed in the original.

"Dear Friends": Ford Hoffman, letter dated September 18, 1957, Dot Wilkinson Collection.

19. The Pain of Loss

"On the field, Catcher Wilkinson": "A Female Yogi," *Sports Illustrated*, October 17, 1960.

"A series of operations this year": Arnott Duncan, "Wilkinson, Rohrer All Stars," *Arizona Republic*, Sunday, July 16, 1961.

20. Turning the Page

WILKINSON UPSETS LADEWIG!: Abe Gutierrez, "Wilkinson Upsets Ladewig," *Arizona Republic*, April 27, 1962.

"Phoenician Dot Wilkinson took": "Dot Wilkinson Takes Thriller in WIBC Match," *Arizona Daily Star*, April 27, 1962.

"Kay urged me to enter": Frank Gianelli, "Dottie May Reject Check," *Arizona Republic*, April 29, 1962.

"Phoenix's unheralded Dot Wilkinson": Abe Gutierrez, "Wilkinson Wins Queens Crown," *Arizona Republic*, Saturday, April 28, 1962.

DOT WILKINSON SOFTBALLER PIN QUEEN: *Dayton Daily News*, April 28, 1962.

JUST PINCH ME, SAYS DOT: *Arizona Sports Journal*, Saturday, April 28, 1962.

INTERNATIONAL BOWLING QUEEN CHAMP: "International Bowling Queen Champ Is Among Nation's Best in Softball Too," Strikes to Spare, *Sacramento Bee*, May 27, 1962.

"That $2,000 check Dottie Wilkinson": Frank Gianelli, "Dottie May Reject Check," *Arizona Republic*, Sunday, April 29, 1962.

"No one can deny now": Abe Gutierrez, "Dottie Showed She Belongs with Best," *Arizona Republic*, May 12, 1963.

"How to Legally Win": "Saturday Serenade for Dot," *Arizona Republic*, August 8, 1963.

"Miss Wilkinson, who has played": "1,500 Pay Dot Wilkinson Tribute," *Arizona Republic*, August 11, 1963.

"We draw hundreds now": Dave Hicks, "Gals Softball Weakly Supported, *Arizona Republic*, Saturday, July 13, 1963.

"Burning candles held by members": Dave Hicks, "Ramblers Pay Rohrer Tribute," *Arizona Republic*, Saturday, July 11, 1964.

"The Orlando Rebels roared": Henry Landress, "Rita Horky's Base Running Nips Phoenix," *Orlando Evening Star*, Thursday, August 27, 1964.

"RAMBLERS, P.B.S.W., 33, passed": Frank Gianelli, "Ramblers Say Adios to Softball," *Arizona Republic*, December 11, 1965.

21. Basking in the Afterglow

"Boy, it's really a nice change": Stormy Irwin, "Wilkinson Honored at All-Star Series," newsletter article, July 1970.

"Dear Miss Wilkinson": Letter on Leland Bisbee Broadcasting Company stationery, January 9, 1963, the Dot Wilkinson Collection.

About the Author

Lynn Ames is the bestselling author of seventeen books. She also is the writer/director/producer of the history-making documentary *Extra Innings: The Real Story Behind the Bright Lights of Summer.* This historically important documentary chronicles, for the first time ever in her own words, the real-life story of Hall of Famer Dot Wilkinson and the heyday of women's softball.

Lynn's fiction has garnered her a multitude of awards and honors, including six Goldie Awards, the coveted Ann Bannon Popular Choice fiction award (for *All That Lies Within*), and the Arizona Book Award for Best Gay/Lesbian Book. Lynn is a two-time Lambda Literary Award (Lammy) finalist, a Foreword Indies Book of the Year Award finalist, a Writer's Digest Self-Published Book Awards Honorable Mention winner, and winner of several Rainbow Reader Awards. *All That Lies Within* was additionally honored as one of the top ten lesbian books overall of 2013. Lynn was honored by the Alice B. Foundation with a Lifetime Achievement Award for her body of work.

Lynn is the founder of Phoenix Rising Press. She is also a former press secretary to the New York state senate minority leader and spokesperson for the nation's third-largest prison system. For more than half a decade, she was an award-winning broadcast journalist. She has been an editor of a critically acclaimed national magazine and a nationally recognized speaker and public relations professional with a particular expertise in image, crisis communications planning, and crisis management.

For additional information please visit www.lynnames.com. E-mail her at lynnamesauthor@gmail.com. You can also friend Lynn on Facebook and follow her on YouTube and Instagram.